Give Yourself
The
Unfair
Advantage

A Serious Practical Guide to Understanding Human Personality that Will Have You Rolling in the Aisles

by
William D.G. Murray

Illustrations by
Ashleigh Brilliant

© 1995 Type & Temperament, Inc PO Box 200 Gladwyne PA 19035-0200 USA

Dedication

To the Teachers and the Children— and to You, the Reader

List the people who have most affected your life for the better. Chances are at least one is a teacher. And if you think about it, one may be a child— including the wonderful inner child within yourself. (Is he or she alive and well? or need to get out and play a little more?)

Pass It On

This book has the power to change your life, and others'. I suggest you may want to pass it on: tell someone— a friend or family member— what you're learning about Type and about yourself, *each day*. Be a teacher; it's the best way to learn. It can also help start others to a new and improved passage through life.

Here's where the child comes in. You'll learn in a more specific, practical and memorable way about your own "inner child." (Yours is different from mine— but every bit as wonderful and powerful!) If you "become as a child," share the wonder, love and caring, you give a gift to the one you share with, and to yourself.

And if you share it with a child— you may change the world! Have fun!

To Dick Deal and Ruthanne Schlarbaum,
two of the brightest, finest, most dedicated and loyal friends and colleagues a man could hope to find in a lifetime. That I have found them all but simultaneously, as it were, and that both have contributed so mightily to this book, is a beautiful gift to me from the universe, and their efforts a gift to you, the reader; for much of the organization, clarity and effectiveness in what I dare to call my words here reflect their work.

Villanova, PA, USA   November, 1994

Contents

Introduction

What would you do if you had information that could dramatically improve the life of everyone in the world who knew about it?

We have that kind of information, and our solution was to put it in this book— with the most powerful, humorous, memorable and compelling illustrations available: Ashleigh Brilliant's famous "Pot-Shots®."

"Give Yourself the Unfair Advantage" is a book that will tell you so much about yourself that you'll wonder why God let you go this far without it.

HOW LITTLE I KNOW ABOUT MYSELF!

ALTHOUGH I'M CONSIDERED A LEADING AUTHORITY ON THE SUBJECT.

© Ashleigh Brilliant 1982   Pot-Shots No 2498

Equally important, after you begin to understand *yourself* so much better, this information will help you identify *other* people's personality styles and motivations. You'll improve your communication, your relationships, and your power and effectiveness with people.

Much of this information was not widely known, understood, or available a few years ago. Most people—including psychologists and psychiatrists— still don't know it, and try to function in the world with remarkable, if understandable, ignorance of themselves and misunderstanding of others. We don't understand our closest family members, friends, people at work, and others in the broader arena.

No wonder we make such a mess out of things! Two people may look at the same scene and see it very differently. We have different ideas of how to define the problem, and even if we see the same problem, we approach a solution differently, have opposing ways to decide what to do about it (or whether it's important to do anything!). When we are, in effect, riding different trains, going different directions, it's no wonder we end up in very different places.

© Ashleigh Brilliant 1974   Pot-Shots No 456

IT WOULD BE EASIER
TO PLAY MY PART IN LIFE

IF I HAD
A COPY OF
THE SCRIPT.

The first step is discovering what train *you* are on, how you got there, and where that train wants to take you. "Know thyself," Socrates said. Alas, most of us don't.

The second step is to find out what train the other person is on, and where it's probably headed—understanding the other guy. There is no better, quicker, simpler way than to understand the basics of his or her personality style ("Psychological Type," as it's called).

This book outlines four simple pairs of choices (like Extravert or Introvert and Thinker or Feeler). With each pair, we all use both, but naturally prefer one, which we use more often. So that one gets better, and becomes characteristic of us. There are 16 possible combinations of these four choices. Each combination is a distinct, often spottable-across-a room style. It's the major part of who we are. We already make decisions about others; Type just lets us do it intelligently!

I WISH
I'D BEEN BORN WITH
AN UNFAIR ADVANTAGE,

INSTEAD OF HAVING TO
TRY TO ACQUIRE ONE.

© *Ashleigh Brilliant 1972*   *Pot-Shots No 363*

Understanding other people better than they understand themselves gives you a real advantage. Perhaps an *unfair* advantage. But hey, some of them already *know* about Type; they have the unfair advantage over *you*, if you don't know.

And when you *both* know Type, it's amazing how much *better* the communication can be. **Type reduces unnecessary conflict.** (There will still be differences of opinion, conflicting views; but even those will be much easier to deal with.)

As with any powerful information, Type can be used for good or ill. There's always a concern when you empower someone as this book does. We see it as a significant long-term benefit. If it's a potential weapon, it is a help both as a positive weapon for good,

6

and as a strong defense against "the bad guys," whoever they may be.

There are some important "Caveats" or warnings about using Type knowledge, summarized on page 236. Remember that Type is a *well-person* tool, and is not meant for diagnosis of mental problems. This book is meant to be educational, not prescriptive. And it is only an introduction; there is much more to Type than we can include here. We encourage you to connect with others interested in Type (see page 139) to discuss and continue learning some of its deeper aspects.

You will learn some things about yourself here that, at some level, you already knew— but never quite so clearly or in such depth. You will also discover some new things that, upon analysis, you will realize are true, and you'll wish you'd known them years ago.

I HAVE TO LIVE WITH MYSELF,
SO I HAVE TO TOLERATE MANY THINGS I DISLIKE ABOUT ME.

© Ashleigh Brilliant 1980   Pot-Shots No 1956

You will also learn some things about your less-developed side— those parts of yourself that are not so strong or well-developed. They may or may not be "weaknesses," but they will probably never be anywhere near as powerful as your natural strengths. The wonderful thing is, that's OK. And understanding why it's so, and that it *is* OK, may be the greatest thing that's happened to you in recent years.

4 Reasons Type is Important for Your Life

There are lots of reasons, as you'll learn. But four key reasons are:

1. Type is a *practical tool* that's *easy to learn, and it really works*.

2. Though not generally known to the public, it's been *tested and validated over decades* (some of the concepts are over two thousand years old). Type, and Type training materials developed by the author and others, are *used regularly* by government, industry, colleges and universities, school systems, churches, counselors and therapists and organizational consultants. There are dozens of psychological theories that deal with or are based on mental *illness;* Type is a *well-person* concept, developed by and for *well* people.

3. Type is a *framework* on which you can hang nearly everything you know about yourself and others, and *understand it all better*. It can be applied to virtually everything human beings do, and has the power to improve it. The *possibilities are limitless*.

4. Type has "a miraculous component," according to a minister friend who's been using Type for decades. *It can change lives, for the better*. Any education can change your life; but learning this much about yourself can *empower* you to change your own life, if you want to. This book may change not only how you see yourself, and others, but your very strategy for defining and obtaining success in life— long-term and short-term.

16 Different Ways to Read This Book

There are at least 16 ways, because there are 16 different kinds of people. You can just read it straight through. Or you can read the end first (but it's not a mystery). Or just skip around. **If you are NOT familiar with Psychological Type or don't know your own Type preference, you may want to turn first to Chapter 6, and go through the "sorter" for a preliminary indication of your own preferences before you read the book proper.** The stronger your choices, the better the chances that they represent your "True Type," i.e., the basic Type you were probably born with.

Now read the book and find out who you are, who your parents are, who you are married to, why your kids aren't like you, and what your boss is all about. Enjoy!

Chapter 1

Extraverts & Introverts

- **E is for Extravert**

- **I is for Introvert**

We all know what an Extravert is, and what an Introvert is, right? Well, sort of. Actually, it's more complicated than most people's general ideas on the subject. When personality experts analyze a person's preferences, they often utilize several subscales — you may operate like an Extravert in some areas, but work more like an Introvert in others.

There are four pairs of **preferences**, like Introvert-Extravert, or Thinker-Feeler, that determine your personal style or so-called "Psychological Type." *We all use all eight, every day*, but we have a natural inclination toward one of each pair. So we use that one

Note: Many dictionaries prefer spelling both "Introvert" and "Extravert" with an O. However, Carl Jung, who put the word in common usage, used an A in Extravert, reflecting the original Latin "extra," meaning "outside, beyond." Jungians and the psychological Type community use "Extravert," as we do here.

more often (it comes naturally). Because we use it more often, we get better at it than its less-used counterpart. So it gets even easier to use that preference— and relatively harder to use the other one we don't prefer. It takes more years for us to get very good at the preferences we don't use so often, and normally they never do get quite as good as the ones we use most of the time.

© *Ashleigh Brilliant 1983*   *Pot-Shots No 2777*

WHICH WOULD BE
THE GREATER PUNISHMENT —
TO BE ALWAYS ALONE,
OR, TO BE NEVER ALONE?

Which would be the greater punishment? That depends: are you an Extravert or an Introvert? Of course, we all can and do use *both* Extraversion and Introversion, every day. But we have a *preference* for one or the other. Extraverts have the most trouble with solitary confinement as a punishment (Introverts may find it rather nice, or at least preferable to some of the other options, and will be better equipped to handle it.) The real punishment for Introverts would be for them to have *no* alone time— especially if they're in the company of Extraverts who want to interact all the time! Actually, of course, *we all need some of each, Extraversion and Introversion, for balance* in our lives, if we are to be fully functional human beings.

10

E is for
Extravert

One important aspect of Extraversion is gregariousness. E's (Extraverts) are people who like people, usually lots of people. They're friendly folks, "people-people." In the high school yearbook, they may have long lists of the activities they joined.

© Ashleigh Brilliant 1969   Pot-Shots No 1621

I PREFER GROUP ACTIVITY BECAUSE, EVEN IF IT'S FOOLISH, AT LEAST I'M NOT THE ONLY FOOL.

When it comes to "group activity," E's are joiners by nature. That's not to say that only E's join anything, because the U.S. is a strongly extraverted culture (75-80% Extravert) and we train people to be Extraverts.

Though Extraverts tend to be generally "popular," they may appear "superficial" to Introverts. That's because Extraverts are "WYSIWYG" (what-you-see-is-what-you-get); Extraverts are

11

Pot-Shots No 4672

very up-front about things. They come at the world with their favorite, and therefore most used and best developed, function— as we'll discuss at length later. That means you see their longest and strongest suit, so you get to know the most important parts of them pretty quickly. Extraverts tend to have lots of friends, though their friendships are more casual, less in-depth than those of Introverts.

Pot-Shots No 1748

Extraverts are enthusiastic, lively, energetic, gossipy. It's tough to be all those things while you're alone, which is why Extraverts usually don't like to *be* alone too much. Enthusiasm falls a little flat with no one to share it with. And how do you gossip with yourself? (Introverts, on the other hand, tend to *love* solitude.)

© *Ashleigh Brilliant 1983*   *Pot-Shots No 2843*

WHY IS
NOISE
SO OFTEN
SO MUCH
MORE ENJOYABLE
TO MAKE
THAN
TO BE
FORCED TO HEAR?

Ashleigh Brilliant

What Extraverts call *enthusiasm,* may just come across as being *too noisy* to an Introvert (especially, for reasons we'll discuss later, an Introverted Senser). There tends to be a higher energy level evident with Extraverts— which can be one way you spot them. This energetic liveliness contrasts with the usually calmer mien of an Introvert.

© *Ashleigh Brilliant 1983*   *Pot-Shots No 2802*

I AM
TROUBLED
BY A FEELING
THAT,
WHEREVER I GO,

I'M NOT
BEING
FOLLOWED.

Ashleigh Brilliant

Extraverts like to initiate things, to introduce people at social gatherings (which they usually enjoy). Their social life is an active

13

one. In fact, Extraverts are "action people" in general. They are likely to be perceived as leaders— or want to be. Partly that's because they're more comfortable with the external environment— the world in general. (Introverts prefer to "live in their heads," so aren't naturally as at home in the outer world; they have to work at it.) Extraverts may also be perceived as leaders because they're more likely to speak up, and speak up quickly, in a situation where leadership is called for. (Even, an Introvert might add, if they have nothing to say.) That's because Extraverts like to think out loud; they talk around the subject until they figure out their real opinion.

© *Ashleigh Brilliant 1982*   *Pot-Shots No 2385*

PLEASE TALK TO ME ~
EVEN IF IT'S ONLY TO TELL ME WHY YOU'RE NOT TALKING TO ME.

Ashleigh Brilliant

The major relationship difficulties between Extraverts and Introverts usually center on the amount of interpersonal communication each wants. Extraverts want more interaction than they get; Introverts want more quiet and alone time than they get. First understanding, and then compromise is needed so that both E and I accept each other and work out a satisfactory arrangement— e.g., "I'm an Introvert, so when I come home at the end of the day you give me 30-45 minutes alone time to 'charge my batteries' (which I've depleted by extraverting all day); then we'll have together time and 'charge your Extravert batteries' (which you've depleted by being alone)."

　　　　　　　　Pot-Shots No 1744

IS IT
MY TURN
YET
TO HAVE
YOUR
ATTENTION?

Extraverts normally *need* that attention from others far more than Introverts do. It's perfectly natural, though it may seem excessive to an Introvert. (Conversely, Introverts *need* that alone time; though that may seem reclusive to Extraverts, it's quite normal for Introverts!) I'll say it again: in an Extravert/Introvert relationship, the major problems are likely to center on the degree of attention paid to each other— the degree of interaction. Start by accepting that difference. Then you can negotiate to get each person's needs met, without feeling something's *wrong* with the other person. (Or that they don't love you any more.)

　　　　　　　Pot-Shots No 2829

A GOOD
FRIEND
IS WORTH
PURSUING ~

BUT WHY
WOULD
A GOOD FRIEND
BE
RUNNING AWAY?

15

A common scenario is for the Introvert to be overwhelmed and drained by too much uninterrupted interaction (Extraverting) and so retreat— behind closed doors, to another room, or just sort of "shut down" right there while the Extravert is present. The Extravert seeks more interaction ("Help!" thinks the Introvert, and retreats further.) The Extravert assumes he's done something wrong, and wants to know what it is; or that the Introvert is angry with him, and he wants to know why; or that the Introvert is upset, and "can I help?" "Yes, leave me alone!" just seems to confirm the Extravert's assumption, so he persists, making things worse, until the Introvert *does* get angry enough to drive him away. Peace at last! But at what price?

© Ashleigh Brilliant 1985   Pot-Shots No 3194

I AM A PERSON OF MYSTERY ~

THE MYSTERY IS WHY I TELL EVERYBODY SO MUCH ABOUT MYSELF.

We mentioned that Extraverts are talkers and like to gossip. They are also more likely to talk openly about themselves and their own thoughts and feelings. They are easy to get to know, and tend to be more openly emotional than Introverts. (For Extraverts who are also Feelers, this is *doubly* true.) Often it's just a matter of needing to "talk things through,"out loud, with someone else. Not just "think" them through, as an Introvert might do.

Pot-Shots No 4762

WHEN YOU SAY SOMETHING WITHOUT THINKING,

IT MAY REVEAL YOUR TRUE THOUGHTS.

Extraverts in fact *do* tend to THINK OUT LOUD. Often they *need* to. As someone said, "I don't know what I think about this until I hear what I have to say about it." Remember the old saying, "Engage brain before starting mouth?" For Extraverts, starting mouth *is* how they engage brain! But this can get Extraverts in trouble, because they may blurt out something they later wish they hadn't said (or revealed).

On the other hand, what an Extravert says first when "thinking out loud" about something may *not* be her true feelings about it— just one thought among many possibilities. The final decision (after she's heard herself think) may be very different. The initial "revelation" may not be a revelation at all, and it may be unwise to assume it is.

17

Pot-Shots No 2557

YOU DON'T HAVE TO SAY ANYTHING IMPORTANT:

JUST BREAK THE SILENCE.

Ashleigh Brilliant

Extraverts tend to be auditory people. That is, they may prefer speaking to writing, making a phone call to sending a letter. They may find a natural skill in dictating rather than writing down what they do write, and may do well to work on that skill (even if they have to transcribe their own dictation).

Pot-Shots No 3053

DOING IT WRONG FAST

IS AT LEAST BETTER THAN DOING IT WRONG SLOWLY.

Ashleigh Brilliant

Extraverts are doers, which means they tend to want to take action: even it's the wrong thing, do *something!* (Good judgment, as Ogden Nash said, comes from experience, and experience comes from *bad* judgment!)

And right or wrong, Extraverts tend to do it quickly.

© *Ashleigh Brilliant 1969*   *Pot-Shots No 125*

TAKE COURAGE!
WHATEVER YOU DECIDE TO DO, IT WILL PROBABLY BE THE WRONG THING.

Extraverts are not always right in their decisions, but they act (often quickly, as noted above), learn from the results, and adjust before acting again. They are always adjusting their course, just as an airplane flying cross-country is "off course" 90% of the time, but always adjusting, and making rapid progress toward its destination.

Extraverts eventually get it right, and are often very successful. The key is not to give up; keep correcting for error, or taking action again! With most successful Extraverts (and many Introverts!) that persistent (adjusted) action is the key to success. Type may be useful to help understand the reasons for failure, so that the next course of action may lead to success.

Pot-Shots No 2192

IT'S HUMAN TO MAKE MISTAKES~

AND SOME OF US ARE MUCH MORE HUMAN THAN OTHERS.

Sometimes Extraverts run out of time, money, patience, friends, or whatever, and have to admit failure— which they are unlikely to call it. (It was just a learning experience!)

EVERY SUCCESSFUL PERSON HAS HAD FAILURES

BUT REPEATED FAILURE IS NO GUARANTEE OF EVENTUAL SUCCESS.

Pot-Shots No 12

Pot-Shots No 3002

THE SUREST WAY TO LEARN IS BY DOING IT~

BUT OFTEN, THE LESSON IS: DON'T DO IT!

Or they may try something totally different. (And if that doesn't work, adjust and try again.)

Pot-Shots No 3830

LIVING IS LEARNING

BUT THERE OUGHT TO BE AN EASIER WAY.

There *should* be an easier way (Introverts tend to think it all through before acting— which has its benefits!) but Extraverts tend to be experimenters, and keep operating the way they know best. Trial and error. Or "testing." *Learning by experience.*

21

Pot-Shots No 4111

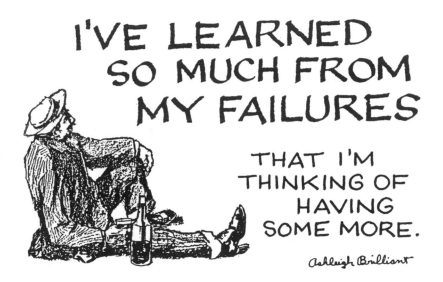

I'VE LEARNED SO MUCH FROM MY FAILURES

THAT I'M THINKING OF HAVING SOME MORE.

Ashleigh Brilliant

In fact, we all need to learn to be more balanced— use our natural skills expertly— but also be able to use the other, less-developed side of our personality well enough when it's called for. Extraverts should (and normally will) remain action people (and all the other E traits) but need to develop their less-preferred Introversion so that they can call on it when necessary, think things through before acting when that's called for, silently polish what they are going to say before saying it, and so on.

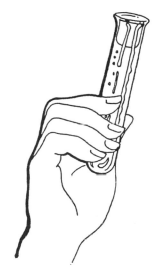

WHAT WE CALL EVOLUTION

MAY SIMPLY BE GOD'S WAY OF LEARNING FROM HIS MISTAKES.

Ashleigh Brilliant

Maybe God is an Extravert! (Ah, there's a speculation for an entire new book!)

I is for
Introvert

　　　　　　　　　Pot-Shots No 463

I LIVE
IN A WORLD
OF MY OWN,

BUT VISITORS
ARE ALWAYS
WELCOME.

Introverts are like a mirror image of Extraverts— they tend to prefer the opposite of what the Extravert prefers. The Introvert tends to prefer one-on-one communication to groups (let alone crowds!), and have deep friendships with a few, rather than easy acquaintance with many people.

© Ashleigh Brilliant 1982   *Pot-Shots No 2659*

As we said, Introverts tend to avoid crowds. At a party, they often find a quiet corner, and carry on a long, deep conversation with one person, while the Extraverts are "circulating."

© Ashleigh Brilliant 1985   *Pot-Shots No 3269*

Introverts are deep people ("still water runs deep"). They're worth getting to know— though it may not be easy. It will take time,

25

because I's require time for the in-depth connection they want. They aren't satisfied with a superficial acquaintance; if that's what the other person wants, odds are the Introverts aren't interested. They limit the *number* of friends, but often have loyal, lifelong friendships, a blessing some Extraverts may miss out on.

MOST OF ME IS BENEATH THE SURFACE

SO DON'T BE AFRAID TO TAKE THE PLUNGE.

© Ashleigh Brilliant 1985   Pot-Shots No 3944

Importantly, an Introvert tends to introvert the part of himself that is his "longest and strongest suit"— his best-developed function, whichever it may be. It is directed inward because he's an Introvert, and it's best developed in part because Introverts spend more time introverting than they do extraverting. So it gets more exercise, and gets stronger. But only those closest to the Introvert get to see much of this side of the person. So as you get to know an Introvert, don't be surprised if you're surprised! You may discover things you never suspected at first acquaintance! The "real person" is very different than most people think— and the Introvert isn't going to tell you that up front! But the longer you know them, the better they get.

AN OCCASIONAL SMILE

IS
ONE WAY
OF
PREVENTING
ICE
FROM FORMING
ON YOUR FACE.

Ashleigh Brilliant

Pot-Shots No 4436

What's really going on in an Introvert's mind is often very different from what's showing on his or her face (if anything *is* showing!) Don't assume! Don't assume a frown in your direction is aimed at you, or if it is, that it has anything to do with your present behavior; it may reflect consideration of something you did long ago— or more likely it may have nothing to do with you. If you're an Introvert, you need to remember to *display* on your face the smiles you're feeling inside! If you don't, don't expect your friends to mind-read! And, to quote "Prescriptions for Introverts,"* don't punish your friends if they don't respond to the things you haven't said!

* " Prescriptions for Introverts," laminated pocket card, one of a set © 1987 by William D. G. Murray.

I WANT EVERYONE TO BE HAPPY~

AT LEAST HAPPY ENOUGH SO THAT NOBODY COMES BOTHERING ME.

Ashleigh Brilliant

© *Ashleigh Brilliant 1985*   *Pot-Shots No 3320*

Introverts really do *like and need* their solitude. Strange as it may seem to an Extravert, you *can* interrupt an Introvert who is alone in a room saying nothing. In fact, that *may* be worse than interrupting when they're talking. Introverts need quiet at the end of a long day of Extraverting, difficult though the concept may be for Extraverts to understand (and enduring that silence may be even more difficult for Extraverts!)

One
very effective
way to make
everything
go away

is to
go away
from everything.

Ashleigh
Brilliant

© *Ashleigh Brilliant 1979*   *Pot-Shots No 1445*

If you *don't* permit Introverts to get the required alone time, they may take drastic action, and go away to get it. (This can be very scary for Extraverts, as many a country ballad attests— "Ain't nothin' short of dyin', worse than bein' left alone.") This need and their overall calmness can make Introverts appear standoffish. They often appear unexcitable, because they are not about to take action (as an E would be). They are going to take the time to consider the matter before moving on it. This can be frustrating to an enthusiastic Extravert. But it may be exactly what the Extravert needs to balance his or her own natural tendencies! Introverts are deep thinkers, and quiet time is how they process and integrate all they need to, to come up with the powerful and polished analyses and responses that are characteristic of Introverts. Often Introverts attain positions of leadership precisely because they think things through— before they open their mouths.

Pot-Shots No 2556

It's usually advisable for the Extravert to allow, in fact to help insure, the Introvert's quiet time. They are better company when you do.

Pot-Shots No 1120

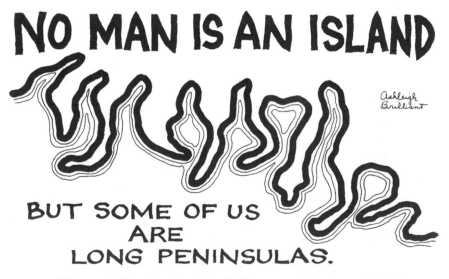

Distance. That's what it feels like to an Extravert. Introverts are truly harder to get to know, because they may be more controlled, especially when it comes to sharing their deepest feelings. (This is also true of anyone who introverts her *Feeling* function— a concept explained later.)

COMMUNICATION WITH THE DEAD IS ONLY A LITTLE MORE DIFFICULT THAN COMMUNICATION WITH SOME OF THE LIVING.

Ashleigh Brilliant

Introverts are of course not the only ones it's difficult to communicate with— and some Introverts are quite easy to communicate with. It really depends on your own four preferences— your "type" or "style," and the type or style of the other person. But Introverts really do communicate *less*. In an organization or relationship they may not communicate enough (while the Extraverts may communicate *too* much!) And Introverts prefer to communicate in writing, especially if it's important. Extraverts would rather communicate verbally, especially if it's important. Obviously, both are liable to miscommunicate the importance of a problem because when an Introvert signals importance by putting it in writing, the Extravert assumes that it wasn't important, or he would have called about it. The Extravert calls about something urgent, and the Introvert may assume it's not important— or it would have been put in writing!

31

DON'T ASK TOO MUCH OF ME, AND DON'T ASK HOW MUCH IS TOO MUCH.

Pot-Shots No 4699

Introverts may actively discourage some communication, especially when they see it as an invasion of their privacy. Extraverts may or may not care for much privacy, and may not even *understand* the privacy needs of their Introvert friends or partners. Social custom of course influences this and other aspects of the Introvert-Extravert dichotomy. In the U.S., Southerners are socialized to be much more extraverted, and northern New Englanders are known for a more introverted style overall.

WHY SHOULD I LET YOU INTO MY PRIVATE HELL?

Pot-Shots No 2875

Remember that impassiveness cuts both ways. The Introvert who doesn't display pleasure even when that's what's going on internally, may also mask hurt, sadness, frustration, even desperation and depression. ("Smile; everyone you meet is fighting a hard battle.") But don't decide an I is depressed because he's not smiling.

Pot-Shots No 2728

SOMETIMES IT TAKES COURAGE TO SAY NO,

OR TO SAY YES,

OR EVEN TO SAY ANYTHING.

Introverts' preference for living inside their head is a powerful one. Though some Introverts learn to extravert most expertly, they may often feel a little discomfort (even panic!) when asked to speak in public. Comedian Jack Benny, who seemed so casual and relaxed on camera, reportedly had to be pushed onstage (literally) even when he was a top star. But remember, when Introverts *do* get to spend the time they need Introverting, they *function* at their optimum level, they *feel* their best, and they *do* their best work. And an Introvert's best work is likely to be deep, thorough, and a real contribution.

BOOKS
HAVE MADE ME
LAUGH AND CRY,
BUT, UNFORTUNATELY,
NO BOOK
HAS EVER
LOVED
ME.

© *Ashleigh Brilliant 1982* *Pot-Shots No 2464*

Introverts are often more likely to be readers (and writers) than the comparable Extravert types—though not always, and some Types (and of course individuals) like to read more than others. And the content and selections may also vary widely with different Types, depending in part on the factors described in the following sections. But their inclination toward reading can give Introverts a tremendous depth of information and understanding, that most Extraverts never discover or appreciate about them.

I WOULD PROBABLY HAVE HAPPIER MEMORIES,

IF I HAD HAD MORE HAPPY EXPERIENCES.

Ashleigh Brilliant

Pot-Shots No 3657

Clearly Introversion is not "lack of Extraversion," and therefore a defect; it is simply a different energy-direction, equally valuable and necessary for all. Ultimately, understanding yourself as an Introvert can be very helpful in terms of self-esteem, self-acceptance, recognizing special gifts you perhaps hadn't identified so clearly, and being better equipped to arrange your life to suit your needs. But there are some potential downsides to being an Introvert *in an Extravert culture.* One is that some Introverts' detached and cautious approach may save them from some mistakes and agony— but may cost them some wonderful experiences and joy as well.

I refuse to live any more of this life

until I'm sure it will be a good one.

Ashleigh Brilliant

Pot-Shots No 1275

Introverts, it is said, refuse to live life until they understand it, while Extraverts don't understand life until they have lived it. Introverts who understand themselves are better able to develop their more venturesome Extraverted side, and may well increase their portion of joy and effectiveness as they do. Similarly, Extraverts who understand *their* own nature can better develop their own *Introverted* side, and find much joy and increased effectiveness also.

Summary— E & I

We live in two worlds:

- **Extraversion**— The outer world of people, places and things.
- **Introversion**— Our inner world of ideas, concepts and images.

We all live in *both* worlds, but we have a built-in preference for one, so we spend more time in that one and focus most of our energy there. We call this (**E**) or (**I**) preference or energy focus an **"Attitude."**

Specific contrasting traits, tendencies and behaviors tend to relate to each. Some may apply to you more than others. You may tend to be an Extravert, but in some ways prefer to operate Introvertedly, or vice versa. That's not unusual. Chapter 6 may help you find your own preference.

Key Words— Extraversion and Introversion*

Extraversion	Introversion
Like group activity, people around, easy warmth with many	Prefer one-on-one, depth of communication with a few
Show you their best side (Dominant)	Show their #2 function (Auxiliary)
Enthusiastic, lively, gossipy	Deep, quiet
High energy level, loud speech	Calmer, softer speech
Like action, initiate it; good greeters	Like contemplation; trouble w/ names/faces
Interaction with people	Need seclusion, alone time
Charge batteries by people interaction	Charge batteries by alone time
Easy to get to know, open, sharing	Harder to get to know, private
Think out loud	Think silently, announce results
May prefer speaking to writing	May prefer writing to speaking
Trial & error, learn by experience	Think through first before acting

---

* Adapted from "Key Words in Type," © 1988 William D. G. Murray

Which do you think you are— Extravert or Introvert? (How about your significant other?)

Prefer Extraversion	Undecided	Prefer Introversion
10	0	10

Chapter 2

Sensers
&
iNtuitives

- **S is for Senser**

- **N is for iNtuitive**

There are two ways we get our information: through our five senses ("Sensing") and with our "sixth sense" or intuition ("iNtuition"— Type experts use an "N" for intuition because we already used I for Introversion). Remember that we all use both ways, but we naturally prefer one, and use it more often.

IS *Ashleigh Brilliant*
LIFE
BETTER
UNDERSTOOD

BY LOOKING AT IT
MORE CLOSELY,
OR
BY STEPPING BACK
FARTHER FROM IT?

© *Ashleigh Brilliant 1985*   *Pot-Shots No 3333*

Sensing and iNtuition give us different pictures of the same scene, like two different lenses on a camera— closeup or telephoto. iNtuitors see the forest, Sensors see the individual trees...and the veins on a leaf. Each preference gives us a different input, and may lead to a different understanding of life. Ideally, we get some input from both; but usually we lean on the one we trust more, and just "go" with what it tells us, for better or for worse.

S is for
Senser

If we rely on what our senses tell us, we get up-to-the-minute, here-and-now factual data on the real world. What do we see? We see what's really there. And we get pretty good at observing— every detail. What do we hear? What's making noise right now... and we get pretty good at identifying sounds. What do we smell? What's there (or was recently), and we may have sensitive noses. Taste? We may also have well-trained taste buds, savoring every morsel, identifying subtle herbs and spices in the sauce. Touch? Sensers may have very sensitive fingertips, as a sculptor who can feel tiny imperfections in the marble he is working with.

MY MIND AND HEART SOMETIMES GIVE CONFUSING MESSAGES,

BUT
THE CALL
OF MY STOMACH
IS ALWAYS
CLEAR.

Ashleigh Brilliant

Pot-Shots No 2489

Here it is in a nutshell. Sensers are attuned to their bodies, listen to their hunger pangs (iNtuitors often don't even notice what they're eating, after the first bite or so, and don't notice other messages from their bodies, such as pain or fatigue).

There's only one thing more beautiful than a beautiful dream,

and that's a beautiful reality.

Ashleigh Brilliant

© Ashleigh Brilliant 1979   Pot-Shots No 1615

Sensers are connected to reality. They're observant, sensible, realistic, matter-of fact. Realists. Bottom-line types. Dreams are nice, but what can we realistically get done?

STATISTICALLY, THE ODDS AGAINST REALITY ARE OVERWHELMING ~

~ WHAT DOES THIS SAY ABOUT STATISTICS?

Ashleigh Brilliant
SANTA BARBARA

© Ashleigh Brilliant 1989   Pot-Shots No 4789

Sensers *believe* what their senses report. Their sensory databanks are usually complete, accurate, and detailed. They can and do trust them.

If Reality's an illusion,

how do we all happen to be having it at the same time?

Ashleigh Brilliant

© Ashleigh Brilliant 1988   Pot-Shots No 4560

Sensers are sensible. Common-sense is their middle name. The world's greatest theory is nothing if it doesn't fit with everyday experience. (I once taught physics at the Air Force Institute of Technology, and had a hard time convincing one experienced, Sensing USAF major that a concrete dam could be as thin as the formulas stated; never mind the theory; he wanted any dams *he* was involved with to be several *times* that thick! Sensers, as we say, are "concrete" people.)

THE THINGS
I FEAR
MAY ALL
BE
IMAGINARY

SO,
WHAT I
FEAR MOST
IS
MY IMAGINATION.

Ashleigh Brilliant

© Ashleigh Brilliant 1981   Pot-Shots No 2217

41

Because Sensers prefer Sensing, their iNtuition is not so well developed. This means that, as with any part of us we don't develop well, when we *do* use it, it acts as if it were a little child— even though the other parts of us may be quite grown up!

Imagination comes from the iNtuition, which is not so well developed, and may in fact be repressed, put down, even feared and ridiculed, as the previous picture shows. The imagination shows us what might be— in the future. So it's a *future* function, not a present, here-and-now one.

DON'T LET LITTLE THINGS UPSET YOU,

OR YOU'LL HAVE NO TIME TO BE UPSET BY BIG THINGS.

© *Ashleigh Brilliant 1988*   *Pot-Shots No 4660*

Good advice. For a Senser, who tends *not* to be a "big-picture person," the details— little things— are usually well dealt-with, but the attempt to look at the total picture or the future configuration of things, involves iNtuition, and thus may provide a distorted view.

BEHIND
THE BIG
QUESTIONS
LIKE:
WHAT IS LIFE?

ARE OTHER
IMPORTANT QUESTIONS
LIKE:
WHAT IS
FOR DINNER?

Ashleigh Brilliant

© Ashleigh Brilliant 1988   Pot-Shots No 4464

All this detailed factual focus tends to make Sensers practical, "do it" types, with a focus on practical applications, on things
rather than theories. Future "pie in the sky" may or may not happen.
But pie on the plate right now definitely satisfies my present needs.

Ashleigh Brilliant

CHANGE
ENOUGH
OF
THE
LITTLE
PICTURES,

AND
YOU'LL FIND
YOU'VE CHANGED
THE BIG PICTURE.

© Ashleigh Brilliant 1983   Pot-Shots No 2882

Funny thing about focusing on details: if you deal with them
all, you do change the big picture. We need to use our sensing to deal
with the details, to achieve our iNtuitive "vision."

Pot-Shots No 3904

How beautifully put! While iNtuitives consciously focus on finding meaning in their lives, Sensers may just do what needs to be done day by day, and *there is their meaning*. Why waste time wondering about what can't be seen (or heard, touched, etc.), and what we probably can't do, when there isn't enough time to get done all the things we want to do, or should do, and probably can do?

Pot-Shots No 4185

As always, the Senser wants details. The facts. The complete story, told *in order*, from start to finish. No iNtuitive flashbacks, please. Recreate the experience (that's what "facts" are). Sensers want certainty— but it must be realistic certainty, and the facts will establish that. "God is in the details," as Carl Jung put it.

THINGS WERE MUCH BETTER,

BEFORE THEY MADE ALL THE IMPROVEMENTS.

Pot-Shots No 4849

Sensers are often conventional folks who don't much appreciate change; they prefer the status quo. If it ain't broke, don't fix it. This is especially true of Sensing Judgers ("SJ's").

WHY ARE LITTLE GENTLE CHANGES

NEARLY ALWAYS PREFERABLE TO BIG SUDDEN ONES?

Pot-Shots No 4677

Sensers do make improvements, but they tend to be an ongoing series of small incremental improvements, not a total sea-shift. That's more conservative, and ultimately can have a great cumulative benefit. But it's not "pizazz." It may miss some totally new technology. (No matter how you improve the process of making buggy-whips, your market is going to be overtaken and passed by the automobile!) That's why Sensers need iNtuitives— as every Type needs its opposite— for balance. You can get this balance either in the form of another person who is different, or by tapping into your own inner resources and using the less-preferred side of your own personality.

© *Ashleigh Brilliant 1979*   *Pot-Shots No 1467*

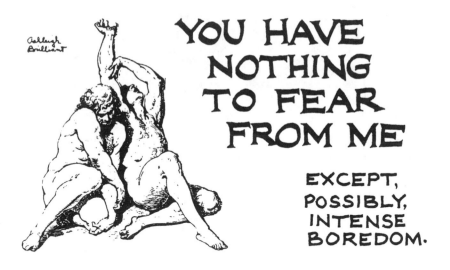

YOU HAVE NOTHING TO FEAR FROM ME

EXCEPT, POSSIBLY, INTENSE BOREDOM.

iNtuitives may sometimes see Sensers as boring, because Sensers may not be interested in the same things as iNtuitives. This is often true of younger iNtuitives, especially if they have not yet begun developing their own Sensing side very well. Sadly, it can also be true of Sensers at times, especially when they are in the grips of their own "shadow side," including an undeveloped iNtuitive function. Sensers don't see many options, but usually they don't need to. However, if they are in a really bad situation— boring, or even hurtful— they may, given the limited options they see, feel really depressed, or at least "wake me when it's over," perhaps said stoically with a wry sense of humor.

Another reason Sensers may appear boring to iNtuitives is because Sensers tend to be conventional, and may resist change. A more positive way to look at this is to see Sensers as "stable." The US has about 75% Sensers and 25% iNtuitors (some say 80-20). Can you imagine the chaos if we had 75% iNtuitives wanting to change everything all the time, and only 25% Sensers to hold them back and make them re-check the facts about the new bridge before demolishing the old one?

© *Ashleigh Brilliant 1980*   *Pot-Shots No 1985*

I WAS GOING
FROM THE PAST
TO THE FUTURE,
BUT SOMEHOW
GOT PERMANENTLY
TRAPPED
IN THE PRESENT.

Ashleigh Brilliant

Sensers are here-and-now people. Their time sense is focused on the present. iNtuitors focus on the future, Feelers on the past, Thinkers on a linear past-present-future time frame. (Isn't that logical?) Sensers try to enjoy the present. However, Sensing Judgers (SJ's) only allow themselves to do this *after* their work is responsibly completed. Sensing Perceivers (SPs) try to enjoy the present by making work fun.

47

Pot-Shots No 2760

I'VE LOOKED AHEAD, I'VE LOOKED BEHIND —

BUT HERE AND NOW SEEMS TO BE WHERE EVERYTHING IS HAPPENING.

The Sensing Perceivers (SP's) are the quintessential, "What's happening?" people. SP's seem to have the most fun, right now! (N's are looking to the future, and miss much of the present; SJ's have responsibilities that prevent their taking time out, or at least prevent their enjoying it!)

Pot-Shots No 2931

THE PAST HAS RETIRED;

THE FUTURE'S NOT READY ~

SO, THE POOR PRESENT MUST DO ALL THE WORK.

OUR ONLY HOPE FOR THE FUTURE IS TO LIVE IN THE PRESENT.

Pot-Shots No 4832

In terms of time sense, it sometimes seems this way. Most of the world's work is done by present-oriented Sensers. That's because they are 75-80% of the population, of course. But in general, as Isabel Briggs Myers once told me, future-oriented iNtuitives are "thinker-uppers," and here-and-now Sensers are "getter-doners," handling the practical hands-on part with grace, skill, and perseverance. (Often without as much credit as they deserve.) Don't take them for granted!

THE ONLY THING THAT MAKES THE PRESENT SEEM TOLERABLE

IS THAT THE FUTURE LOOKS EVEN WORSE.

Pot-Shots No 3806

This is the Senser's motto, and it's a valuable one— within limits. The present handled well can help deliver a good future. But it also helps to plan... which requires using our iNtuitive side to look at the future.

© *Ashleigh Brilliant 1988*   *Pot-Shots No 4517*

I'M GLAD THAT ONLY NOW REALLY EXISTS,

BECAUSE CERTAIN PARTS OF THE FUTURE DON'T APPEAL TO ME.

That's what often happens when Sensers try to use their iNtuition: it's not well developed— in fact, it's likely to be quite childish in its development— so the information it provides is faulty. When they look at the future, they see only a few possibilities, all bad! Gloom and Doom. One iNtuitive lovingly nicknamed his Sensing wife, "Vog," for "voice of gloom." Together they made a good balance. (He tended to see an infinite number of future possibilities, most of them rosy— see iNtuitives, next page.)

N is for iNtuitive

SEEING IS BELIEVING —

I WOULDN'T
HAVE SEEN IT
IF I HADN'T
BELIEVED IT.

      Pot-Shots No 1025

While Sensers don't believe what they can't see, iNtuitives ignore what they can see, and look for the deeper meaning, read between the lines, intuit new possibilities or opportunities beyond (sometimes antithetical to) what actually *is* right now. iNtuitives have that "vision thing," as President Bush's weakness was sometimes described (he's *not* an iNtuitive!) When a woman told the great artist, "Mr. Turner, I've never seen a sunset like that!" he replied, "Ah, Madam, but don't you wish you *could*?!" Sensers start with what they have in the present, then try to make it better. iNtuitives start by designing a future they'd like to see, then work toward it, sometimes ignoring apparent present constraints.

© *Ashleigh Brilliant 1979*   *Pot-Shots No 1440*

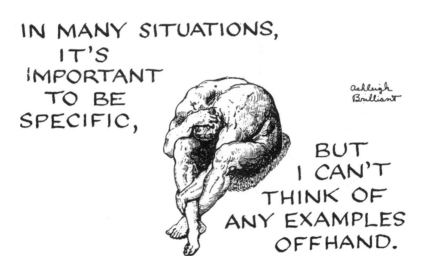

IN MANY SITUATIONS,
IT'S
IMPORTANT
TO BE
SPECIFIC,

BUT
I CAN'T
THINK OF
ANY EXAMPLES
OFFHAND.

Sensers look at the present facts. iNtuitors look at "future facts" (a meaningless concept to Sensers). Where Sensers are literal, iNtuitives are figurative, dealing in metaphors, symbols, paradigms. The iNtuitive function in the brain basically combines different things— whether they appear to have any reasonable or appropriate relationship or not. They take disparate words like "paperclip" and "sculpture," and say,"Aha! I'll do a sculpture of a paper clip!" (It's been done.)

iNtuitives see the big picture— not the details (Sensers are better at those). They'll admit that specifics are sometimes important, but their brains literally don't tend to store that kind of information unless they force them to (e.g., for the test tomorrow in a class taught by a Senser) or unless those specifics are necessary for something that's important to the iNtuitor. If they want to be a doctor, they'll learn every bone and muscle in the human body. But in technical subjects, rather than learn all the formulas, they may prefer to learn the basics really well (e.g., in physics, learn the formula, "F= ma") and derive everything else from that when they need it.

WHY IS IT THAT I'M MOST AWARE OF MY BODY ONLY WHEN IT'S NOT WORKING PROPERLY?

© Ashleigh Brilliant 1985   Pot-Shots No 3958

iNtuitors are not "observant" in terms of details, though they may notice things that are different, or patterns, or intuit meanings in whatever they do notice; they see between the lines, what isn't there. Generally, because they intuit well, they don't do their Sensing very well. That means iNtuitives tend not to tune in to their bodies. They don't listen to what the body is trying to tell them— not just sights and sounds. And especially aches and pains, which some, especially ENPs, may not notice until they go to bed at night and turn off the lights, and there's nothing more they can see "out there." They may then become instant hypochondriacs, because they can intuit lots of possible causes for each little ache, many of them fatal. But in the morning they awake and don't notice them any more, and go on with their lives (helpful unless the pain was something they really *should* have checked out!).

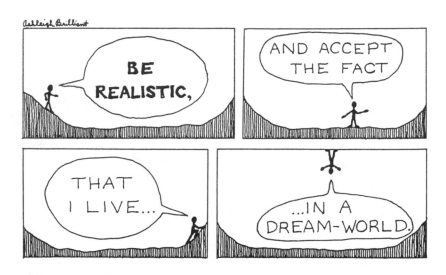

　　　　　　　　Pot-Shots No 348

iNtuitives are known for their imagination, their ingenuity, their wonderfully creative new ways of solving problems. The opposite of the matter-of-fact Senser, they may sometimes appear to "do it the hard way"— or at least the complicated way— because they are so complex in dealing with situations in their minds. Sometimes their solutions need a little reworking to bring them into the context of reality (Sensers can help here).

　　　　　　　　Pot-Shots No 1831

I consider Reality
an intrusion
on my
dreams.

iNtuitives really don't like to pay more than lip service to reality and its limitations; they work in a world where there are no such constraints, and it's much more interesting and enjoyable! As long as we're dreaming, there are no limits; "when you dream, dream big." Don Quixote's "impossible dream" had much goodness and beauty in it— though he needed practical Senser Sancho Panza to intervene when reality became too pressing.

I haven't told myself that I'm getting older, because I hoped I wouldn't notice.

© Ashleigh Brilliant 1981   Pot-Shots No 2088

Aging and ultimate mortality (an iNtuitor's way of saying we are all going to die) are two facts that iNtuitives learn to ignore with amazing skill. (Also the ticking biological clock— one mature woman I saw wore a T-shirt: "Oh, Hell. I forgot to have a baby!") As N's often do, they may still achieve their desire with a remarkable last-minute effort— in her case, perhaps assisted by modern medical science.

I EXPECTED
DIFFICULTY
IN DOING
WHAT CAN'T BE DONE,

BUT NEVER
REALIZED
THAT IT WOULD BE
IMPOSSIBLE.

© Ashleigh Brilliant 1985   Pot-Shots No 3827

iNtuitives sometimes *do* do the impossible. (Because they ignore facts such as the fact that it's impossible to do that, N's are the most likely to attempt the "impossible" in the first place.) And surprisingly often, considering the odds, they succeed, often by discovering a totally new way of doing it. iNtuition is what powers the inventors, poets, writers, and entrepreneurs, those who pioneer and embrace the new before most people realize it's even an option.

THANK GOD
FOR
MAKING
REALITY,

AND FOR GIVING US
MEANS OF
ESCAPING FROM IT.

© Ashleigh Brilliant 1981   Pot--Shots No 2132

iNtuitives have a wonderful, (usually) positive way of escaping from reality: intuition. In fact, they develop sort of "automatic pilot" methods of dealing with much of reality. This trait allows them to observe the overall scene, without paying much attention to details unless it is consciously required of them (and even then, they find it hard to stay focused for long on the detail level). iNtuition allows them to make major changes in reality, at least long-term; and since those changes are underway, and thus practically accomplished (in the mind of the iNtuitive), there is no need to be upset by (or even pay much attention to) the discomforts, pains and problems of the present. They can be put up with — by ignoring them.

I don't always succeed, but some of my failures are better than many people's successes.

Ashleigh Brilliant

© *Ashleigh Brilliant 1979*   *Pot-Shots No 1573*

iNtuitives are likely to be inventive, as we said. When asked to improve a process, they are likely to project the "perfect" process, and figure how to approximate that— even if it would mean a 300% improvement over the present version. The 200% improvement they actually achieve may seem like "failure" to some, though it's far better than the 6% a year improvement achieved by the traditional Sensing approach: start with the known facts, the present way, and try to improve each step, incrementally. That's the safe way. And over time this Sensing approach may well win the race, like the proverbial tortoise vs. hare— especially if one of the iNtuitives' radical changes doesn't work, or is counterproductive.

Best of all, of course, is to use the best of *both* sides! Keep making incremental improvements, while *also* staying open to the radical new possibility. This uses both our iNtuition, and our Sensing sides— or the talents of both the iNtuitive and Sensing group members.

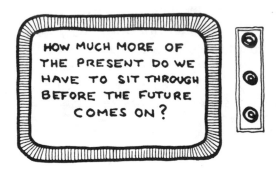

© Ashleigh Brilliant 1967   Pot-Shots No 16

Where do you live isn't a geographic question for iNtuitives; it's a chronological one. iNtuitives live in the future. They may hardly pay any attention to the present. The implications of this fact, as any iNtuitive will immediately realize, are legion. Sensers are here-and-now, short-term focus people; iNtuitives are concerned with the long term, their plans for the future; they can put up with a great deal in the present so long as they see a future worth working toward. They may need to work at living more in the present, smelling the daisies, tuning in to their sensory input— while still appreciating their ability to see into the future, create something new there, and make it happen.

Pot-Shots No 2091

I BELIEVE THERE IS A FUTURE SOMEWHERE AHEAD,

EVEN THOUGH NOT THE SLIGHTEST EVIDENCE OF IT EXISTS.

Ashleigh Brilliant

The Senser wants evidence. "Just the facts, Ma'am," as Sergeant Friday of the TV show, "Dragnet" used to say. iNtuitives see the outlines of the future in the slightest hints in the present. They would deny that no evidence exists: it appears writ large in neon lights to iNtuitives, and they marvel that others can't see it!

Pot-Shots No 2538

I WON'T REACH MY LIFE'S GOAL TODAY,

BUT, WITH LUCK, I MAY REACH YESTERDAY'S GOAL SOMETIME TOMORROW.

Ashleigh Brilliant

One problem iNtuitives may have stems in part from their seeing the future too clearly. They think it will happen soon, while in fact the rest of the world is years slower than they can imagine in embracing the obvious new wave of the future, whatever it may be. iNtuitives (especially Dominant iNtuitives) are notably bad at estimating how long a project will take to finish. A general rule of thumb for iNtuitives is to estimate the best you can, then triple it and add fifty percent. That's your deadline. Then tell the world a week later than that, but aim to beat the first one. (It can work if you don't take on five such projects simultaneously.)

I WOULD NATURALLY PREFER CERTAINTY,

BUT IT SEEMS I WILL HAVE TO SETTLE FOR HOPE.

Pot-Shots No 3810

It's hard enough to be sure of the *past* (in the play, "Rashomon," several characters narrate the same events— and everyone has a different story of what happened). Often there's small consensus as to *the present*, and there are an infinite number of possible futures. So no matter how "certain" an iNtuitive seems to be of the particular future he or she is envisioning, there is normally a realization deep down that it is in reality just a hope—albeit one with a very high probability of coming true. (At least in some form.) iNtuitives need to be flexible in enacting their programs, and sometimes even in adjusting their goals, as they go along.

Summary— S & N

There are 2 things the brain does:
- Gets information (Perceiving)
- Decides what to do about it (Judging)

There are 2 ways we Perceive, or get information:

• **Sensing**— using our 5 senses (sight, hearing, touch, smell, taste) to give us the present facts about the world. We know, because we can see it hear it, touch it, etc.

• **iNtuition**— a "sixth sense" that uses instant mental interconnections to show us the meaning of things. We know, but we don't know *how* we know; it's a "hunch" we can rely on.

We all use *both* Sensing and iNtuition every day, but have a *natural preference* for one, which we use more, so it gets stronger and more reliable.

Specific contrasting traits, tendencies and behaviors tend to relate to each. Some may apply to you more than others. You may tend to be a Senser, but in some ways prefer to operate iNtuitively, or vice versa. That's not unusual. Chapter 6 may help you find your own preference.

Key Words— Sensing & iNtuition*	
Sensing	**iNtuition**
Strong capacity in 5 Senses	Strong 6th Sense- hunches reliable
In touch w/ reality, the facts- what *is*	In touch w/ possibilities, imagination- what *could* be
Take things literally	Take things figuratively, symbolically
Concrete	Abstract
Precise	Approximate
Practicality- what is do-able	Creativity- attempt the impossible
Sensible, commonsense, applications	Vision, dreams, stories, wordsmiths, theoretical knowledge
Details, see trees, veins on leaf	Big picture, see patterns, see forest
Status quo, tradition	Change, new way
Incremental improvements	Radical reinvention
Simplicity	Complexity
Present time focus, here & now	Future time focus
May seem boring to iNtuitives	May seem impractical to Senser
75-80% of population	20-25% of population

*Adapted from "Key Words in Type," © 1988 William D. G. Murray

Which do you think you are— Senser or iNtuitor?

Prefer **Sensing**	**Undecided**	**Prefer** **iNtuition**
10	0	10

Chapter 3

Thinkers
&
Feelers

• T is for Thinker

• F is for Feeler

There are two ways we make our dreams come true— that is *decide* what we are going to do: with our heads or our hearts, our logical Thinking Judgment, or our personal values-based Feeling Judgment. As with Sensing and iNtuition, we use both every day, but have a natural preference for one, which we use more often and develop sooner and more powerfully.

Both are rational logical processes, but use different criteria for judgment: the objective rules of logic, for Thinkers; and subjective personal values, for Feelers. (Thinkers may not see Feelers' criteria as valid at all, since they are not necessarily logical; Feelers may not see Thinkers' criteria as valid at all, since they do not necessarily take into consideration the human part of the equation.)

I'M READY TO TACKLE
MY PERSONAL PROBLEMS ~

BUT
SHOULD I
ATTEMPT
A POLITICAL
OR A
MILITARY
SOLUTION?

© *Ashleigh Brilliant 1985*   *Pot-Shots No 3694*

This can be read, "should I use my Feeling judgment or my Thinking judgment?" Not that political solutions always notably consider the Feeling function, or values (other than the important value of getting re-elected). Someone once put it, "use your Thinking on your car, and your Feeling on your family." How true. Kicking the car door may be briefly satisfying, but costly and ineffective if the problem is the carburetor. And using logic on a child in an unfeeling way may be tragically counterproductive.

Again, the key is to remember that *we all have both* Thinking and Feeling sides, and *we must learn to use each* in the appropriate situation. That's what true Type development—human development— is about.

The two ways we perceive (S & N) and the two ways we decide (T & F) are called our 4 *"functions."* We all use all 4, but have a preference for one of each kind (one perceiving and one judging function). In fact, we have a *1-2-3-4 order of preference* that is determined by our Type. We generally do our *best* work when we use our #1 ("Dominant") function; we have most difficulty using our #4 (least-preferred or "shadow function"). See page 148 and Chapter 8, "The Shadow Knows."

63

T is for Thinker

LET'S PUT THE BLAME WHERE IT BELONGS: ON SOMEBODY ELSE.

Pot-Shots No 1083

Thinkers are great critics, and good at figuring out what's wrong with something. Or someone. They may be quick to lay blame—though not so quick to assume it when it falls on them. This is usually not done in a personal way, nor is it meant personally (though Feelers find that hard to believe). It is just a simple rational conclusion from their logical analysis of the situation. Thinkers (or Thinking analyses) figure out what kind of O-ring design will let the Space Shuttle be launched safely. In some situations, when other concerns (funding, publicity, etc) override the logic of the Thinking analysis and ability to find flaws, there can be trouble. (In other situations, the reverse is true. Thinkers overriding important Feeling considerations can also wreak havoc!)

Feelers, on the other hand, may be too quick to assume blame that should not rightly fall on them. They may in effect apologize for something someone else did. "I'm sorry," from a Feeler, means I'm sorry that things are less than wonderful for you. It may sound as if it's the Feeler's fault.

YOU WILL
NEVER KNOW
HOW MUCH
I HAVE ENJOYED
ALL YOUR CRITICISM.

ashleigh Brilliant

Pot-Shots No 497

Thinkers hold down the "tough" end of William James' tough-minded/tender-hearted spectrum. They can take criticism as well as dish it out, and generally not take it personally as Feelers are wont to do. They see criticism as necessary feedback if they are to improve. *Thinkers tend to be the tough-minded types who can see things through, and do the things Feelers find hard to do.* Most of the corporate turnaround artists who come in and fire 40% of the work force are probably Thinkers, who see that action as the only logical solution; otherwise the whole company could go under and 100% would lose their jobs. They don't dwell on the hardships of each family displaced by their downsizing. This is not to say that Thinkers enjoy inflicting pain, or fail to consider such effects, or are not affected by the human problems resulting. Simply, having decided what is necessary, they tend to be more comfortable with proceeding to do it.

Thinkers, especially iNtuitive Thinkers, are also likely to consider the criticism of a fool to be praise indeed, and it won't bother them as it might a Feeler. Criticism from a respected expert may well be greatly appreciated, as a student artist learns to appreciate the teacher's comments that help the learner improve.

You're not angry with me, are you, just because I did something foolish which hurt you deeply?

© Ashleigh Brilliant 1982   Pot-Shots No 2472

Thinkers are forever stepping into this one. They hurt feelings and don't realize it. Or even if they realize it, they seem to underestimate by several orders of magnitude just what that means to the other person, especially if it should be a Feeler. They really didn't *mean* to hurt feelings. (They may even have intended something nice, but didn't understand some key bit of illogic which tripped them up once again.) Thinkers thus may appear hard and cold to Feelers, because (a) Thinkers are not so much aware of and in touch with their *own* feelings; it is likely to take them time to get to the point of even being conscious that there *is* a feeling there. (b) Thinkers find it hard to *express* these feelings even when they do recognize them. (For one thing, the moment may well have passed; and bringing it up again later is seldom easy to do, especially without a mediator, if the situation has deteriorated from uncomfortable to very difficult.) (c) Thinkers are also usually not so well tuned to the feelings of others, either past, current, or inferable future . Thinkers are often described as "tough-minded and effective." The tough-minded comes more easily; true effectiveness in many cases comes when the Thinker matures enough to be conscious of the Feeling factor of the equation, and build that into the solution.

66

HOW CAN I GIVE YOU MORE LOVE WITHOUT HAVING TO GIVE YOU MORE TIME?

© *Ashleigh Brilliant 1979*   *Pot-Shots No 1600*

Thinkers tend to be straightforward in their communication (Feelers might say: tactless). Thinkers may "tell it like it is," honestly, and be surprised that some unspoken assumption (e.g., about what priority the love relationship has for the other person) gets them in trouble. The Thinker might be perfectly willing to give more love, if a way could be found that would not cut into his or her other activities, mental or physical. More likely, he (60% of Thinkers are male) just doesn't understand the importance of the matter as measured by the other person's *Feeling* valuation. The Thinker may even have heard the words but not truly heard them— or discounted them as illogical, and ignored or forgotten the point entirely. Sometimes the first voice the Thinker will notice is that of the spouse's lawyer. Or when the Feeling boss tells them they are fired.

The Thinker needs to pay more attention to the Feeling side, of course. But the Feeler also must recognize the *value* of the Thinker's honest unvarnished opinion, hearing it for what it is, not taking it personally.

```
LOVE EXPRESSES ITSELF IN STRANGE WAYS --

    Think of that

        The next time

            I attempt to destroy you.
```

ashleigh Brilliant

Pot-Shots No 640

Thinkers enjoy a good argument, and often will play devil's advocate just for the fun of it, even taking a position with which they disagree. Once they have taken a position, even for the sake of argument, they want to be "right," i.e., they want to win— even over a child or a loved one (the Feeler may well let the other person win, just so they'll feel good). To the Feeling mate of a Thinker, this competition is usually not the fun the Thinker thinks it is, and the Feeler may withdraw to lick wounds and consider finding a new mate who will provide harmony rather than "disagreement."

This is another area where simply understanding what is going on can take 90% of the sting out of the situation. Type can be an invaluable tool to help people understand this dynamic.

WHY DO I HAVE SO MUCH TROUBLE FORCING PEOPLE TO LIKE ME?

Ashleigh Brilliant

Pot-Shots No 1570

Thinkers, especially Dominant Thinkers, may recognize themselves here (those mature enough to care much about the matter). The Thinkers may not see themselves as "forcing," but it may feel that way to a Feeler. Most people like to be liked, if possible. (Though Thinkers are likely to say they'd rather be respected.) But a Thinker's natural style may involve force, coercion, or at least heavy-handed persuasion, which is tough on the Feeler.

It's not all that simple, though; this quote may also at times fit Feelers, for whom Thinking is the fourth or "shadow function." Thinking as a fourth or shadow function can be overweening and power-oriented, using power to coerce— even to coerce pleasantness. Often this is to avoid the discomfort of having to deal with disharmonious Feeling situations: "Be kind and gentle or I'll kill you." Wars (not just preparedness) to insure peace. Adolf Hitler was probably a Dominant Feeler, for whom Thinking would be the shadow function. He applied logic in a childish way (but with grownup force) to implement what he saw as the logical solution to Germany's problems.

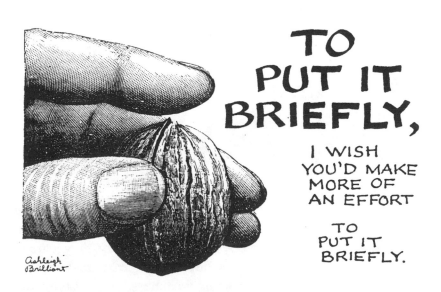

TO
PUT IT
BRIEFLY,

I WISH
YOU'D MAKE
MORE OF
AN EFFORT

TO
PUT IT
BRIEFLY.

© *Ashleigh Brilliant 1981*   *Pot-Shots No 2352*

69

Thinkers pride themselves on brevity. They like to say things once. Period. Once should communicate. *Feelers, on the other hand, may not be speaking so much to communicate information, as simply to make a connection* with the other person. So repetition is no problem to the Feeler. (iNtuitors may repeat several times, each with some subtle nuance of difference *meant* to enlighten, not enrage.)

We once received a manuscript from a Dominant Thinker, and the Feeler editor could scarcely resist the temptation to add interesting, informative— but basically repetitive— material. Fortunately, he recognized what was happening, and left it alone except where something was truly needed (the Thinking author's descriptions of Feeling were, understandably, not as clear and complete as his descriptions of Thinking).

Brevity can be one way to identify a Thinker, if you are "Type-spotting.™"

DON'T BE AFRAID TO HURT MY FEELINGS:

ALL YOU RISK IS MY UNBOUNDED RAGE.

© Ashleigh Brilliant 1976   Pot-Shots No 946

Thinkers do have feelings. But they may not believe they have permission to express them, so they generally suppress them, and try not to show them. Big boys/big girls don't cry, they learned at an early age. Often the feelings they express least are the tender ones, ones they may associate with "weakness." "If I show any feelings, I lose," one Thinker said. (And if I see you displaying any, *you* lose!) They may, however, have permission in their mind to express anger, or at least be unable to control that one feeling at times. So the feelings that have been pushed down so long build up pressure, and come out unexpectedly in a volcano of rage, verbally or physically expressed. This may convince them that feelings are a dangerous thing, and should be controlled even more forcefully— which works until the pressure builds up again.

[Note carefully that "feelings" or emotions are *not* the same as the Feeling *function*, which is the process of making decisions using our personal values rather than logic. However, persons who use Feeling judgment usually are more in touch with their feelings or emotions, and those who prefer Thinking judgment often get less experience dealing with (or even recognizing) their feelings or emotions. *The two are often related, but are not the same thing.*]

IF YOU
BOTTLE UP
YOUR FEELINGS
INDEFINITELY,

EVENTUALLY,
THEY'LL ALL
GO SOUR.

© *Ashleigh Brilliant 1977*   *Pot-Shots No 1152*

As we said, feeling must out, eventually. "Murray's Law" says that bottled up feelings will always explode on the scene at the worst possible moment of the most important negotiation of the most important relationship or business deal. It's like a boisterous child that is locked in the basement so he won't embarrass the parents in front of guests, or inconvenience their own interactions.

71

They leave him down there for years sometimes, feeding him generously, but never letting him see the light of day. He grows. He becomes a strapping young man, at last strong enough to break loose. And he comes out swinging his chains, wreaking havoc with the good china and the good relationships. Inevitably. Those who most value control, lose it most painfully.

What to do? Let the kid out to play. I repeat, *play.* Recreation is a wonderful outlet for emotions. People who haven't expressed a positive emotion to their loved ones for years freely admit they "love" the Red Sox or the Yankees. People who would rather die than express even a mild negative emotion in a close relationship admit they "hate" the opposing coach or linebacker. Spectator sports aren't as good as participation, but they're better than nothing. "A feeling a day keeps the shrink away." Better yet, two or three feelings. Don't be afraid of joy; it deserves equal time! Joy comes in Introverted and Extraverted varieties, though only the latter is contagious.

But don't stop there. Practice your real Feeling judgment. Spend some time thinking about what's really *important* to you in your life— past, present, and future. What do you really value? There are "Values Surveys" you can take, lists of significant values that will almost certainly be *prioritized* differently by you and anyone else who does the same exercise with you— mate, child, co-worker. There are usually enough values that the random chance of two people agreeing exactly is miniscule. That's OK. Generally, it's more important to recognize where you and the other person are coming from generally, than that you agree exactly. Start by being aware of your own value system—which are more and which less important? Apply this *consciously* to your next decision. Even if you don't ultimately decide based on that input, recognize it is important information. If you decide logically, but in conflict with your values, you will have an internal conflict or dissonance that, unrecognized, can eat you up or sabotage your decision. Understanding the situation helps (sorry, it doesn't make it *easy*!).

I AM NOT UPSET,

AND WILL CONTINUE TO DENY HOW UPSET I AM UNTIL I CALM DOWN.

© *Ashleigh Brilliant 1977*   Pot-Shots No 1355

Denial is a primary tool for protecting ourselves against having to deal with our least-preferred or 4th function* (among other things). Thinkers may not recognize they are "having a feeling" at the time they are having it. They may not recognize the power of the feeling; even as they are expressing it by screaming at you, they may insist they are perfectly calm. Understanding this can be their first step to improving their life and the situation. And for others to understand it can take much of the acrimony out of such occasions and relationships. It doesn't make it fun to be shouted at, but you can handle it without so powerful a reaction when you know that it's not meant as a personal attack, that they don't really hate you, that they and/or you are not evil people. (Be careful that your newfound calm doesn't, in some situations, just enrage them more! Let them know in advance, if possible, about this aspect of Type, and give them time to cool off— perhaps make an appointment to discuss the matter later.)

* Page 148, Chapter 8, and your own Type description will tell you more about your 4th function and how it affects you.

LET US
ALWAYS BE
FRIENDS,

BUT
LET US NOT
ALWAYS BE
REQUIRING
EACH OTHER
TO SHOW IT.

© Ashleigh Brilliant 1982   Pot-Shots No 2431

Thinkers are usually not enthusiastic about displays of emotion (this is compounded if they are also Introverts). Feelers (especially Extraverts) may be more interested in expressions of emotion, especially warm feelings from friends or loved ones. Understanding and some negotiation is often needed to allow such a pair to get along comfortably for both. (There is a story about the laconic Vermonter who said of his wife, "I told her when I married her that I loved her, and if I ever changed my mind, I'd let her know.") (Especially) if she was a Feeler, this was *not* an entirely satisfactory relationship!

IF YOU ALWAYS TRY TO BE LOGICAL,

YOU PROBABLY WON'T EVER HAVE MUCH SORROW,

OR MUCH FUN.

Ashleigh Brilliant

Pot-Shots No 4438

Thinkers try to be impersonal in their judgments (that's what "Thinking judgments" are). This may spill over into the rest of their lives, and they may try to be logical and impersonal in virtually everything! As it says, they miss a lot of joy and pain that way. Which is to say, sometimes they miss life. They may even choose to do so consciously— often out of fear of repeating a past painful experience— but more often it's an unconscious Feeling choice they need to be made aware of. (Thinkers do make Feeling decisions, but often they are not even aware they are doing so!) Those whose best function is Thinking, often have trouble with, deny or suppress their Feeling side, for fear they cannot control it should they start to let it be expressed. They prefer their Thinking, as being more level; and though there will be some conflict and bumping into others, it will all be more controlled. It is like an amusement park, where the roller-coaster (F) is very different from the bumper-cars (T)— F has more ups and downs, is more exhilarating, feeling out of control at times, perhaps dangerous-feeling. But you don't really fall out. Everyone should have the experience!

75

DISASTER CAN SOMETIMES BE AVOIDED

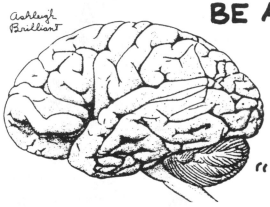

Ashleigh Brilliant

BY USE OF A NEGLECTED PROCESS CALLED "THINKING".

© Ashleigh Brilliant 1980   *Pot-Shots No 2000*

Thinkers apply reason to everything they do or consider doing. Many laws include a test of what a "rational man" (person) would do—i.e., they assume people will make decisions based on a Thinking judgment. And Thinking types are, or try to be, just and impartial, eminently fair— as they see it. ("Fair" can have a different meaning to a Feeling person.) The Thinker tries to use cause-and-effect analysis to provide some foresight of what will happen **if...** a much-needed talent!

WHAT I MOST DISLIKE ABOUT REALITY

IS THAT IT DOESN'T TRY HARD ENOUGH TO MEET MY EXPECTATIONS.

© Ashleigh Brilliant 1983   *Pot-Shots No 2909*

Thinkers may expect reality to be logical. That's only reasonable, right? Wrong. Relationships are seldom reasonable, even those between two Thinkers, if they are important (a Feeling judgment)! If Thinkers are to be effective and get what they want in life, they ultimately must face up to the need to appreciate their own and the other's Feeling function. A frequent scenario: if you're a Thinker, find a highly logical career— engineer, scientist, attorney, economist, accountant or chief financial officer— and bury yourself in it for years. Be a workaholic. Avoid your spouse and kids, where all those uncomfortable Feeling transactions occur; limit yourself to the financial or scientific ones. After 20 years you may be highly successful, wealthy— and alone and miserable. And if you're really unlucky, convinced you are right and they are unreasonable. I say unlucky because this attitude may prevent your accessing your own vital Feeling function (or delay this work until your next marriage falls apart), and will certainly make negotiations more difficult and your children's lives more painful. Yours, too. (In a divorce situation, if you've been totally one sided, you may actually *ease* the emotional burden on your, by now, hated spouse, because you will be seen as so unreasonable as to justify your aggrieved spouse's viewpoint, regardless of the facts— to the extent objective "facts" exist in such situations.)

As with any attempt to develop a less-preferred function, start off easily— if you're a Thinker, by letting your Feeling function decide some things that won't be disastrous no matter how they're decided. Recreational applications are always a good place to start (see Chapter 8 on the shadow function, and Appendix I on Energy Direction).

F is for Feeler

YOU DESERVE SOME PRAISE, SO, HERE IT IS :—

PRAISE

Pot-Shots No 559

Often the first noticed and most obvious difference between Thinkers and Feelers is the Feeler's tendency to praise others while the Thinker is good at finding out what is wrong and criticizing it. Feelers will always look for the good things to compliment, even if their overall evaluation is negative (this is good management style as well). You catch more flies with molasses than with vinegar, as my mother was fond of saying.

Pot-Shots No 847

Guilt. Feelers often seem to have a special guilt-collection apparatus that collects all the guilt for miles around, regardless of whether they have any reasonable connection to it. It all stems from the Feeler's tendency to take things personally, to see situations as if from the inside. Feelers feel involved, even if they're just watching TV. (Thinkers feel as if they're watching from the outside— even if they're part of the scene themselves.) Feelers may be quite forgiving— of others, but when it comes to themselves, they pick up all their own guilt, and half of everyone else's. (Thinkers, in contrast, may encourage this by laying the blame on others, not themselves.)

I HAVE NOTHING DEFINITE TO APOLOGIZE FOR:

I'M JUST SORRY ABOUT EVERYTHING IN GENERAL.

Pot-Shots No 2177

    This is another way of looking at it: Feelers are attuned to everyone else's feelings, and sympathize or even empathize when others have problems. They can imagine how terrible the other person must be feeling, and they feel bad, too. So they do, in fact, apologize for things they had nothing to do with. Or so it sounds; they *say*, "I'm sorry." In fact, they *are* feeling sorry, and are expressing that feeling, if not exactly apologizing and taking full responsibility for your difficulty (though it may seem that way). If you feel bad, they feel bad.

MY EAR
IS ALWAYS
OPEN FOR
APPRECIATION,

BUT FOR
CRITICISM,
YOU HAVE TO
MAKE AN
APPOINTMENT.

© *Ashleigh Brilliant 1982*   *Pot-Shots No 2583*

Feelers like, seek, and try to create harmony. So it's natural for them to be the Great Appreciators, as we said earlier. In fact, when it comes to giving criticism, even much-needed, long-overdue criticism, they may have a struggle. It doesn't come naturally. They appreciate *being* appreciated, too, and expect to be. They expect that people just naturally should appreciate other people, even for little things. They may not much appreciate (that's a gentle way to say "be outraged") when others, usually Thinkers, fail to appreciate, let alone— Heaven forbid! — *criticize!*

A Japanese businessman, being praised by an American for his firm's efficiency, told the American that (approximately), "Efficiency is not our goal; our goal is harmony. When we create real harmony, efficiency happens."

THE BEST KIND OF SELFISHNESS

is the kind that gets selfish pleasure from helping other people.

© *Ashleigh Brilliant 1983*   *Pot-Shots No 2945*

Feelers usually like to be helpful— even in small things. They are— or can be — tuned in to the other person (*any* other person, but especially someone close to them). They may also expect the same attitude of others, if they are to be considered first class human beings. In a sense, helpfulness is a value, and though Feelers decide based upon their own subjective value systems, not *all* Feelers may hold helpfulness in such high esteem— but that's the way to bet! (Remember, there are helpful Thinkers, too— but they are more likely to value being right over being helpful. And they may be helpful for their own logical reasons, e.g., relating to what they may expect to get from it.) The Feeler is more likely to be helpful because s/he values helpfulness, feels better when being helpful...gets selfish pleasure from it, if you will. And people who value helpfulness and harmony greatly may be *very* unsympathetic (sometimes cold, even spiteful) toward another who is not helpful, or who disrupts harmony or is insensitive to others' needs. (If you're not kind and gentle, I'll nuke you!) This is the "shadow side" of the warm feeling function. We may see this reaction in Thinkers working on their Feeling function, as well as in Feelers themselves.

Ashleigh Brilliant

ALL I ASK
IS THAT YOU
CONTINUE
INDEFINITELY
TO LET ME
TAKE
ADVANTAGE
OF YOUR
GOOD
NATURE.

© *Ashleigh Brilliant 1988*   *Pot-Shots No 4417*

These helpful Feelers, ever focused on harmony, can be easy to take advantage of, and individuals and entire institutions often do. This is why professions or careers that are generally attractive to Feelers (e.g., nursing, social work) are notoriously underpaid. The Feelers are working for a cause in which they believe, and they tend to value what they are doing for how much it helps others. This "psychic pay" or satisfaction is often the major part of their total remuneration; they may be expected to sign on for peanuts, and continue working with few and small raises. Until they learn to value their own efforts and learn assertiveness skills, this is likely to continue. It is a major reason some women have promoted the idea of "comparable" pay for "comparable" work. Whether that concept is workable or not (how *do* you compare apples with bicycles?), the *real* problem relates to the Feeling-Thinking difference and the kinds of careers to which each gravitates. (One of the important contributions of Type is helping individuals to find the kinds of work they are most likely to enjoy, be motivated by, and thus succeed in.)

WHAT GOOD
ARE YOU
IF YOU DON'T
NEED ME?

Pot-Shots No 1028

"People who need people are the luckiest people in the world," the song says. It was perhaps referring to Feelers (and to Extraverts, to a degree). Feelers are the "*people* people." Folks with natural skills in dealing with the human equation, all the not-so-logical but powerful factors in so many important decisions— the area where logic doesn't help very much, and in fact can be a serious drawback at times. Andrew Carnegie said, "I will pay more for the ability to deal with people, than for any other talent a man may possess." Perhaps the reason Feelers are good at this is their focus on and *need* for other people. As Alexander Pope said, "The proper study of mankind is man." (He didn't say "person," for it wouldn't scan.)

I DON'T LIKE TO BE ACCUSED UNJUSTLY

OR EVEN JUSTLY.

Pot-Shots No 1338

One of the soft spots for Feelers is their often extreme dislike of discomfort and disharmony. They may simply turn off or ignore input they find unpleasant. Denial. If I don't like the idea, it can't happen! [Ah, but it does, and it always comes as such a surprise to the Feeler, who failed to consider the logical (Thinking) *consequences* of his or her actions!] Feelers in a group may subtly (or even bluntly!) exorcise all Thinkers from the group, and lose the valuable contributions (or warnings) they might have otherwise benefited from. Younger Feelers especially may tend to avoid using their 3rd or 4th function Thinking, as being troublesome, unreliable, and standing in the way of what the Feeler wants to do. Mature Feelers may have learned to use their Thinking side, accept it, though it be unpleasant, and learn from it. They may eventually learn to see their Thinking side as a friend, as desirable or even essential in the long run, if uncomfortable short-term.

I HOPE
NOTHING IMPORTANT HAPPENS
IN THE PRESENT

WHILE I'M ABSORBED IN
TRYING TO UNDERSTAND
THE PAST.

© *Ashleigh Brilliant 1979*   *Pot-Shots No 1619*

The past. That's where Feelers live, especially "Dominant Feelers," people for whom Feeling is their Dominant or most preferred function. At some level, they are trying to relive the past in the present, or plan for its re-creation in the future. We all remember most easily events to which we attach strong emotion. Feelers may attach subjective emotional content to much that goes on in their lives, even minor events or observations. ("That was a funny look that just passed over Jim's face. I think he doesn't love me any more.") Actually, Jim was suppressing a burp. But his expression is forever stored in Sue's mind, to be replayed and re-evaluated as other "evidence" comes in. She may not even hear him say, "I love you" right now— though there's a fairly good chance *that* might get through her reverie.

LOOK OUT!

YOU'RE STEPPING ON MY VALUES!

Ashleigh Brilliant

Pot-Shots No 1676

Values are the basis for Feelers' decision-making. They often have a very well-developed system of values: what is good, what is right, what is important— to them. Sometimes it's what's important to mankind (or womankind); sometimes it may in fact be quite selfish. It may not appear logical to a Thinker. But two logically conflicting values may be held in seemingly paradoxical inconsistency by a Feeler, and so long as the conflict is not brought unmistakeably to the fore, he or she may go on enthusiastically supporting both poles.

Remember: "Feeling" in Type theory does *not* mean "emotion." It means *making decisions using one's personal values as the criteria.* Both T and F use a rational system, but with different criteria. Feeling criteria may seem quite illogical to a Thinker, who uses the *laws of logic* as the criteria for judgment. Note that the process is the same logical process, but with different criteria. The laws of logic are universal, so all Thinkers tend to come up with a similar solution, given the same input. Not so with Feelers, for whom their own value systems are each different.

THE REALLY GREAT PEOPLE

ARE
THE ONES
WHO
KNOW HOW
TO MAKE
THE
LITTLE PEOPLE
FEEL GREAT.

Ashleigh Brilliant

© Ashleigh Brilliant 1980   Pot-Shots No 1682

Feelers are focused on people, truly *interested* in people. They tend to develop sensitivity to other people's problems, and are willing to invest *time* in other people. Feelers like to please people, even in little things. (Thinkers tend to want to be *right*, even in little things.) Feelers remember the little personal things about their friends. If you love a Feeler, you should, too.

Pot-Shots No 2188

WHY IS THERE ALWAYS SUCH A POWER STRUGGLE

WITHIN THE MOVEMENT FOR PEACE AND FRIENDSHIP?

Ashleigh Brilliant

We mentioned the importance of *values* to Feelers. They base their actions on their value systems. Plural. Different Feelers have different value systems. And few if any are based on logic, as are the *principles* that drive Thinkers' decisions. They may agree on the problem, but not on the solution— because they are aiming at very different goals. (Two Thinkers, on the other hand, *if* they see the same problem, are more likely to agree on "the *only* logical solution," precisely because they agree on using the laws of logic to decide.) Logic problems tend to have one right answer; values problems have an infinite number. And each individual is convinced that his or her values are the only "correct" ("good," as opposed to "evil") ones, and should be enforced on the rest of the world for its own good, like it or not. The end doesn't justify the means, *except* with any very important end that a Feeler's values are pushing toward. In that case, it often feels OK to ignore facts, other solutions, other people's values, the laws of logic and obvious (at least to everyone else) disastrous consequences. A handful of people with unshakeable conviction in their mutually agreed upon values can be indeflectable as they steamroller everyone in their path. (They may be Feelers— or Thinkers whose "shadow side" Feeling has run amuck!) This is why some of the organizations most founded on principles of love and caring for humanity can be

89

incredibly cruel and vindictive in dealing with employees or others whom the caring leadership comes to see (for whatever reason) as opposed to the "correct" values. They can break laws and get into personally disastrous situations because they are blinded by their powerful value systems, which somehow excuse whatever action their values (often their blind rage at someone who is not being kind or thoughtful enough!) urge them toward. The confirmed pacifist may become violence-prone if a cherished cause is threatened. A devout Christian may want to be, and want everyone else to be, Christ-like; and when they are not, comes a powerful urge to crucify them! The principle applies equally to any religion or spiritual focus or "good cause."

And this just applies to those folks who mean well, who focus on the other person more than on themselves. In addition, there will always be people who focus first on themselves—"what's in it for me?"— and will try in any situation to grab control, as often happens with a revolutionary movement conceived and led initially by idealists; before long they are fighting over narrow differences in their values and goals or directions for the cause, and the door is opened for a cynical opportunist (e.g., a Stalin) to take it over.

© *Ashleigh Brilliant 1985*   *Pot-Shots No 3630*

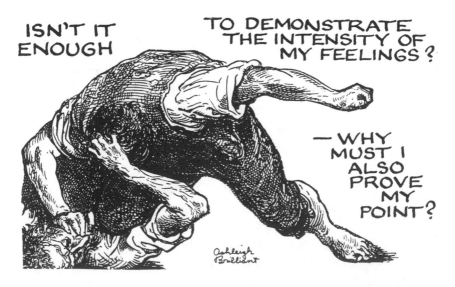

ISN'T IT ENOUGH TO DEMONSTRATE THE INTENSITY OF MY FEELINGS? —WHY MUST I ALSO PROVE MY POINT?

Feeling judgments aren't likely to seem logical (i.e., make any sense at all) to a Thinker because they aren't logic-based. Logic is irrelevant when you're in love, right? Well, Feeling judgments are a bit like that. When we want something badly enough, we may trample the facts and ignore the consequences. Damn the torpedoes! Full speed ahead!

Sometimes, of course, Feeling judgments succeed while perfectly logical Thinking judgments fail— usually because the latter didn't take into consideration the human factor. "It was all indisputably logical that she should stay— but she left me!" "There is no rational way we can offer more than a 50¢ an hour increase." But the workers go out on strike. Sometimes the intensity of the feelings *does* prove the point; the Thinker ignores such input at his or her peril. Illogical or not, feelings and Feeling judgments are facts to consider in the logical equation if we are to understand a situation.

Of course, as we discussed earlier, the difference between Sensing and iNtuition means that two people may observe different "facts," and perceive different possible solutions, before we even *start* to think decisions.

Summary— T & F

To recap, there are 2 things the brain does:
 • Gets information (Perceiving)
 • Decides what to do about it (Judging)

To repeat, there are 2 ways we Perceive (Chapter 2), or get information:
 • **Sensing**— using our 5 senses (see, hear, touch, smell, taste) to give us the present facts about the world. We know, because we can see it.
 • **iNtuition**— a "sixth sense" that uses instant mental inter-connections to show us the meaning of things. We know, but we don't know *how* we know; it's a "hunch" we can rely on.

91

There are also 2 ways we Judge, or make decisions:
   • **Thinking**— deciding objectively, using the laws of logic as the criteria. A rational process.
   • **Feeling**— deciding subjectively, using personal values as the criteria. Also a rational process, but the criteria are different.
Very Important Note: 60% of men are Thinkers; 60% of women are Feelers. So the 40% of males who are Feelers and the 40% of females who are Thinkers have to "swim upstream" against societal expectations. This is initially a disadvantage, but can ultimately become an advantage.
   Much of what is commonly thought of as "masculine" vs "feminine" is simply "Thinking" vs "Feeling" preferences which correlate 60% with sex, so skew results that don't account for Type.

Key Words— Thinking & Feeling*

Thinking	Feeling
Great critics, find flaws	Great praisers, find what's good
Tough-minded, can reprimand, fire	Soft-hearted, can be taken advantage of
Like to argue, disagreement OK	Need harmony, avoid disagreement
Want to be right even in little things	Want to be helpful, even in little things
Logical, objective, impersonal	Values-based, subjective, personal
Time focus is linear, past-present-future	Time focus is the past— try to recreate its good feelings
Impartial	Loyal
May hurt others' feelings unintentionally	May be intolerant of people who hurt others' feelings, even unintentionally
Place blame	Accept/collect guilt
Straightforward, tell it like it is	May deny facts if not harmonious
May control others to do the "right" (reasonable) thing	May control others to do the "good" thing (what's good for people involved, what I want)
May see Feeling as weakness	May try to avoid Thinking altogether if possible, see it as cruel/ heartless

---

*Adapted from "Key Words in Type," © 1988 William D. G. Murray

Which do you think you are— Thinker or Feeler? (How about your significant other?)

Prefer Thinking	Undecided	Prefer Feeling
10	0	10

Chapter 4
Judgers
&
Perceivers

- J is for Judger
- P is for Perceiver

LET'S ORGANIZE THIS THING

Ashleigh Brilliant

AND TAKE ALL THE FUN OUT OF IT.

Pot-Shots No 986

    The movie and play, "The Odd Couple," depicted the difference between Judging and Perceiving types. The Judging folks like to get decisions made; then they'll feel comfortable about things. Therefore they organize everything to that end. They make lots of little decisions quickly, and are fond of saying, out loud or to themselves, "Let's get this organized!" They enjoy organizing; they certainly enjoy the feeling that things are organized! (And they hate it when they aren't!) They're the "clean-desk crew." They tend to have surfaces clear, or with a minimum of objects sitting out; no clutter! Piles of papers, if they are visible at all, are likely to be squared off neatly, and aligned perfectly parallel to the edges of the desk or table. But it's deeper than just the "clean-desk-look." That's only an indication that the person probably organizes every aspect of life (or tries to). Order is something Judgers come by naturally. (And Perceivers have to work at.)

Judging types hate surprises, because they want to know they are in control (or at least that *someone* is). They enter into a situation expectantly; that is, they will have some sort of *expectation* and make a plan based on it, even if they lack adequate information to have a well-informed expectation. Surprises shatter their illusion of being in control, and throw them off-balance until they can assimilate the new information and develop a new plan. (J's who are "between plans" are in a rough place; be gentle with them!)

But remember, Judgers *do their best work* when they can work in a neat, orderly environment, and in an organized way. A touch of chaos may motivate a Perceiver, but it can unnerve and ultimately demotivate a Judger who's not sold on the idea.

Perceivers, on the other hand, do *their* best work when they *don't* have to operate in a "J" environment, with only one piece of paper at a time on the desk, but can juggle projects, let things get a little untidy (or have a Judger to file and retrieve things for them).

You've now read about the first 3 pairs of choices (E-I, S-N, T-F) and have some idea of your own 3 preferences. When you finish this 4th chapter on J-P, you'll have a good guess as to your own 4-letter Type (one letter for each pair of two choices, e.g., if you prefer Introversion, Sensing, Thinking and Judging, your 4-letter Type is "ISTJ."

Judging-Perceiving denotes how you prefer to *relate to the world*: Perceivers naturally try to *understand* the world; Judgers naturally try to *organize and control* it.

J is for Judger

© Ashleigh Brilliant 1980   Pot-Shots No 1853

Control. The crux of the matter with J's, who love— no, *need*— to be in control. Of their own lives, and sometimes of those around them! Perhaps because they like to handle things in an orderly, organized, step-by-step, one-thing-at-a-time manner, they like to know that everything is all set up so that things will proceed that way. (P's plan, too, but they don't necessarily stick to the plan when they see a way to improve it, nor do they really expect anyone else will, either. Plans are just rough directional indicators for P's.)

95

> *"The year's at the spring*
> *And day's in the morn;*
> *Morning's at seven;*
> *The hillside's dew-pearled;*
> *The lark's on the wing;*
> *The snail's on the thorn;*
> *God's in his heaven—*
> *All's right with world."*
> *Robert Browning, Pippa Passes, Part I*

Robert Browning's poem is a classic J checklist as much as a poem; everything is going according to plan, as should be; "God's in His heaven, all's right with the world" is the powerful conclusion that makes him feel wonderfully safe, secure and comfortable. To a less ecstatic or poetic extent, that's how J's feel when things go according to plan.

HOW CAN WE HAVE A PARADE,

IF EVERYBODY INSISTS ON TAKING A DIFFERENT ROUTE?

Pot -Shots No 3065

Judging folks are the ones who organize the parades of life. (Perceiving types often decline to cooperate, and walk off on their own routes, much to the consternation of the organizers.) Judgers often aren't comfortable with everyone marching in a different

direction (on *their* project, at least); Perceivers aren't usually comfortable marching to someone else's drummer. J's like things fairly
predictable; P's resist predictability with a passion. P's don't need
to be in control— but they may need not to BE controlled!

THE KIND OF
DISCIPLINE
I MOST
RESENT

IS
THE KIND
I IMPOSE
ON
MYSELF.

Pot-Shots No 2325

Discipline is a wonderful word for J's. They are generally
much better able to be disciplined than are P's, unless the P's have
strong motivation (e.g., survival or lust) to force concentration.
While we all have to learn some discipline (at least, or perhaps
especially, *self-discipline*), it just seems easier for J's, who are
naturally more disciplined themselves. P's can learn it, but often
don't until later years, and then only by bitter (expensive) experience.

Military training can be healthy and life-changing when it
teaches some necessary self-discipline to young J's and especially
P's. Though they hate it, resist it, and leave as soon as possible, it
can be invaluable training in developing their "other side," something we all need. Generations of Americans have become better
citizens, developed better earlier, because their military experience
helped develop their "J" side.

97

IF YOUR LIFE'S REALLY FULL,

NOTHING
   YOU
   EVER LOSE
WILL MAKE YOU
      VERY
   UNHAPPY
FOR VERY LONG.

Ashleigh Brilliant

© *Ashleigh Brilliant 1981*   *Pot-Shots No 2317*

Judging types have full calendars, because they plan their lives and live their plans. To meet with them, you may have to set a date weeks in advance. When their lives are in turmoil, they may schedule things even more tightly (especially Extraverted J's), so they don't have much alone time to dwell on their troubles and get depressed, preferring to focus on others' problems short-term. There is a therapeutic logic to this tactic: it keeps them from wallowing in self-pity and allows them to work on their problems slowly. But it can be self-defeating if not enough time is spent working on the roots of the problem. But focusing on other people's problems does give perspective to our own!

Of course, Judgers don't have to be wrestling problems to have full calendars; that's normal for them. They do accomplish a lot in life, because they plan and schedule so well, and so *consistently.* That's the big difference; Perceivers can and do plan, often very well, especially when circumstances force them to. But it's not their natural style, and they are more easily distracted from their schedule than a J, who may seem unable to stop something, once started! Perceivers may achieve things they didn't plan on...

Judging types want to avoid stress; that's why they seek control. (Perceivers, in contrast, may enjoy stress, or at least need some to do their best work.)

Stress = (Problems) — (Flexibility)

If stress equals problems minus flexibility, Judgers focus on minimizing the Problems part of the equation, while Perceivers try to reduce stress by maximizing Flexibility. So Judgers like to get an early start, whether it's catching a plane or completing a project. They try to think of all the problems that may arise and head them off at the pass. "No bad surprises" is an oxymoron for them; *all* surprises are bad to Judgers. (That's a basic principle, but of course not always true; the Judger in me wants to state it as an absolute, but the Perceiver in me requires that I make it clear that there are exceptions, and this is really only a tendency, as is true of all Type principles.)

© Ashleigh Brilliant 1975   Pot-Shots No 802

IF ONLY
I COULD ALWAYS
BE FULLY PREPARED

FOR THE
TOTALLY
UNEXPECTED!

Ashleigh Brilliant

Advance preparation is one way Judgers try to gain control and minimize stress. In school they did their term papers ahead of time, not with a frantic all-night burst the last night before the deadline. At work they plan, organize and prepare for every contingency. They have a Fire Emergency Plan, a Flood Emergency Plan, maybe even a What-if-Everyone-Gets-the-Flu-the-Same-Day Emergency Plan. (As always, the other 3 letters also affect this tendency; ISTJs are probably most likely to carry this to extremes, especially if their least-preferred iNtuition runs away with them.) But overall, it's a very good idea to plan ahead for emergencies. Fire drills save lives. Emergency Plans save businesses. And Judgers are good at seeing that these plans get done.

In short, J's need to have a plan. When it gets upset, they get upset. They're not in a good place until they've figured out a *new* plan; they may be immobilized, grumpy, distracted, or worse. (A Perceiving type's flexibility can be very helpful at such times!)

© *Ashleigh Brilliant 1980*   *Pot-Shots No 1810*

I CAN'T CONTROL
THE PASSAGE OF TIME,

But sometimes, I can control
what happens in it.

Ashleigh Brilliant

Judgers are more structured in their use of time; they use it, it doesn't so often use them.

> *"But at my back I always hear*
> *Time's winged chariot, hurrying near."*
> Andrew Marvell (1621-1678) "To His Coy Mistress"

It may be that fear of death, the ultimate loss of control, is what causes J's to strive to control things. But more likely it's a simpler urge, built in from birth or from early experience that taught J's that control was what worked for them. Perceivers are more likely to move toward more control later in life, reflecting their own experience and training, and sometimes the realization of their own mortality, as one likely Perceiver (Keats) put it:

"When I have fears that I may cease to be
Before my pen has gleaned my teeming brain..."

Perceivers can learn to plan and be organized (to some degree, they must). Judgers, as they mature, must learn to be more flexible, to relax and "go with the flow" more, as Perceivers do naturally.

© Ashleigh Brilliant 1981   Pot-Shots No 2160

PREPARE FOR ETERNITY:

TIDY UP YOUR ROOM.

What can I say? J's *need* tidiness about them to operate effectively, especially on a long-term basis. So they tend to require it of the young children under their control. They may even invest the requirement with a supernatural, eternal conditional overtone. God loves you— *if* you clean up your room. The Lord helps them who hang up their clothes, pick up their toys, etc... until the onset of puberty, when, especially with certain types, the natural bias toward chaos will out, and parenthood becomes increasingly a stressful experience of maddening loss of control. (If too many things are going wrong in the J parent's life, their control needs might require even more control. Almost certainly, unsuccessfully.)

101

Judgers like order in general. Their offices are neat, clean-desk affairs (there may be stacks of papers— but they are *neat* stacks, as we said).

And they tend to dislike distractions or anything that threatens to interrupt or divert them from their planned activity. (Perceivers may enjoy such interruptions).

© Ashleigh Brilliant 1980   Pot-Shots No 1679

IF I ALWAYS DO TOMORROW'S WORK TODAY, THE LAST DAY OF MY LIFE WILL BE TOTALLY FREE.

The list. The plan. The schedule. The diligent effort. J's do have "a little list," as Gilbert & Sullivan put it. Usually written down, sometimes in their head, but they have a list, in priority order, and they do the items on the list. Usually in the order planned, unless something comes up to disrupt the Plan. Then they have to regroup, and are at a loss until they have a new plan figured out. Then it's forward again!

Perceivers have lists, too, but they're more casual about them.

And in a J/P relationship, the P may well be co-opted into working on the J's list of scheduled items, so the P's list doesn't get accomplished.

Pot-Shots No 2575

IT'S GOOD
TO HAVE
STRONG
OPINIONS,
IF YOU'RE
RIGHT,
BUT
NOT GOOD AT ALL,
IF YOU'RE WRONG.

Judgers have opinions. They make judgments. Sometimes those judgments are tentative, sometimes strongly held opinions. But it's hard to tell which is which, because they all sound so decisive! J's *speak* in judgments, in pronouncements, in decisions. It sounds to a Perceiver as if the Judger has considered all the evidence, thought of all the possible solutions, and decided the matter. Period. In fact, the situation may be open for discussion; it just doesn't *sound* that way. One Judger was accused of being "Judge and Jury and hangman all at once," when the Judger thought he had expressed a *tentative* opinion!

Incidentally, this can also apply to *Introverted* Perceivers (IPs), because their strongest, "Dominant" function is always a Judging function (Thinking or Feeling), although it is normally Introverted and they don't show that to the world much.*   An Introverted P is a "closet J." Once they decide, IPs' decisions can seem pretty much "cast in bronze."

* For more on this see Energy Direction Appendix I

Pot-Shots No 2909

WHAT
I MOST
DISLIKE
ABOUT
REALITY

IS THAT
IT DOESN'T
TRY HARD ENOUGH
TO MEET
MY
EXPECTATIONS.

Judging types *do* have expectations, as we said. One aspect of the J preference is the tendency to approach every situation with some sort of expectation or preconceived idea of what is going to happen, what's on the other side of the door you've never opened before. The Perceiver, on the other hand, is likely to approach that same door with an open mind and wondering with great curiosity, just what *is* on the other side?

These expectations extend to people and relationships. J's are more likely to *project* their expectations on the other person, and be disappointed when they do not live up to them. They may or may not have even communicated these expectations to the person who is about to be punished or abandoned should they not fulfil them. The expectations may or may not be realistic. But they are there! When dealing with a J, try to find out those expectations if you can (though they may not even be conscious to the Judger, until after you've failed to live up to them, and they suddenly realize that).

Pot-Shots No 1512

IF I DIE BEFORE DOING EVERYTHING ON MY LIST,

TO WHOM SHOULD I LEAVE THE LIST?

The list, the responsibilities, the things to do. Actually, J's will leave shorter lists than P's will, because they've focused their energies more in the first place (only things likely to get done get on the list). And they've concentrated on doing the items on the list (not adding lots more before the first one is done). And they've probably managed to find help in at least some situations— often help from Perceivers, who never got *their* list done because they were drafted into service doing the J's list.

P is for
Perceiver

I CAN DO ANYTHING I DECIDE TO DO ~

THE ONLY THING I CAN'T DO IS MAKE DECISIONS.

Ashleigh Brilliant

Pot-Shots No 4086

That's it in a nutshell: Perceivers like to perceive; Judgers like to decide. Perceivers want to postpone decision-making until they have lots more facts (if they're Sensers) or lots more possibilities figured out (if they're iNtuitives).

Judgers may decide too soon, without adequate information, because they immediately feel better once a decision is made, even if it's the wrong one. Perceivers may decide too late, because they feel worse after a decision is made, even if it's the right one. Perceivers don't like to see other options cut off any sooner than absolutely necessary.

© Ashleigh Brilliant 1980

I NEVER
HAVE
ENOUGH
TIME ~

SOME
OF MY LIFE
WILL HAVE TO
BE LIVED BY
SOMEBODY ELSE.

We stated earlier that Judgers like to have things done ahead of time, all under control. Perceivers like to have a little pressure to make them do their best work (or even to get it done at all). They are what is called "stress-facilitated." They are the stay-up-all-night-before-the-paper-is-due students. They seem totally unmotivated to get it done on a "normal" Judger's timetable. But come the eleventh hour, they are transformed into a whirlwind of remarkable talent, synthesizing ability and writing skill.

One reason is the Perceiver's tendency to take on more than a normal human being's workload, and promise its completion unrealistically soon (especially when other commitments are considered).

Another is the "inspiration factor." Perceivers (especially iNtuitives) have a need for something to be interesting before they'll bother doing it. Deadlines, as Isabel Myers said, make things interesting. The stress of a time constraint seems to "get the juices flowing" in a Perceiving type. All the facts and possibilities they'd been collecting randomly before, seem to be available and fall into place magically at the last possible moment. Like Indiana Jones in the Temple of Doom, time and again they get through the doorway just before the portcullis smashes down to seal it off. Sometimes they swear (or Judgers make them swear) that next time they'll get it done with a comfortable time margin to spare. But they don't, or even if they do, they continue re-thinking it and want to redo it all at the last minute anyway. Judgers and Perceivers each represent about half the population. But the folks lined up to mail their income taxes just before midnight on April 15 must be 80 or 90% Perceivers!

© *Ashleigh Brilliant 1981*   *Pot-Shots No 2279*

SOMETIMES IT SEEMS MY WHOLE LIFE IS A SURPRISE PARTY.

Perceivers are the casual, laid-back types who welcome interruptions and *love* surprises. Partly that's because they fail to plan, as a Judger would put it. Or do they fail to plan because they love surprises? It may be simply that they can handle practically any situation that arises, as it unfolds, and rather enjoy doing so. So why plan? It doesn't provide them with any advantage, even in the rare case where things actually do turn out as planned.

It can sometimes be extremely helpful to be able to recognize Perceivers vs Judgers. On a recent trip to Mexico, I stopped at a bank to cash some traveler's checks. In Mexican banks, there are different windows for different kinds of transactions. (And long lines at every window.) I couldn't see myself waiting in line, only to find out it was the wrong line, and the signs posted didn't include traveler's checks. So I sized up the tellers, and picked out an obvious Perceiving type. I went to the front of that line, and waited for a moment when she was between tasks, and quickly asked her, in my

108

best pre-prepared Spanish, which was the line for cashing traveler's checks? Without missing a beat or appearing flustered, she nodded to the left with her head and said, "La tercera, senor." (The third.) No big deal; Perceivers don't mind, and even enjoy, diversions. Mission accomplished, I joined the third line and got my funds. If I'd tried to ask a Judger, it might have been much different. She would have perceived it as a real interruption, and for her, it would have been. Odds are she'd have asked me to go to the back of her line and wait my turn to ask the question. If I did persist and ask her, it would have thrown her off from her current transaction, and delayed the others in line, who would not have been happy with the Gringo.

© Ashleigh Brilliant 1980   Pot-Shots No 1960

MY LIFE
IS ALREADY
COMPLICATED
ENOUGH,

Ashleigh Brilliant

WITHOUT
TRYING
TO INTRODUCE
ORGANIZATION
INTO IT.

Perceivers seem to be able to deal with chaos comfortably; they either don't need to organize it to deal with it, or they organize it unconsciously, without needing to put the structure down on paper first. If they are iNtuitive Perceivers (NP's), they somehow synthesize great complexity and arrive at an answer without really knowing how they did it. If they are Sensing Perceivers (SP's), they just pragmatically do what needs doing, one step at a time, to make things work. Judgers, meanwhile, may well be on hold while they develop new plans to reorganize things, before they act. Both are valid approaches, but each of us tends to favor one or the other more often. We really operate better that way. Which is your preference?

© *Ashleigh Brilliant 1982*   *Pot -Shots No 2366*

I INHERITED BEING DISORGANIZED FROM MY MOTHER ~

IF SHE'D BEEN MORE ORGANIZED, SHE'D NEVER HAVE HAD ME.

We keep mentioning organization, which is a major discriminator between Judgers and Perceivers. But Perceivers can and do organize, often very effectively, and Judgers do learn to operate effectively from a Perceiving mode. (In fact, in parenting especially, a Perceiving mode may be easily the best available.)

© *Ashleigh Brilliant 1977*   *Pot-Shots No 1357*

I TRIED TO GET INTO ORGANIZED CRIME,

BUT THEY SAID I WAS TOO DISORGANIZED.

Perceivers will love this Pot-Shot® as a funny comment on their lives; Judgers will enjoy recognizing their Perceiver friends. But remember, Perceivers may well operate better with seeming disorder than they could if there were a Judger requiring them to maintain a clean desk at all times. (The Judger may be happier that way, but s/he will not get the Perceiver's best work.) Organization is in the eye of the beholder.

© Ashleigh Brilliant 1979   Pot-Shots No 1544

I NEED A GOOD DIRECTORY OF HARD-TO-FIND THINGS....

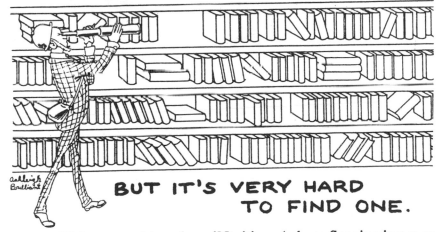

BUT IT'S VERY HARD TO FIND ONE.

This one could apply to iNtuitives (whose Sensing is not as well developed, so they have trouble finding things— even things right in front of them, or things filed in exactly the right place). But it can also apply to Perceivers, who don't always (some would say, never) put things back where they came from. One of the things you're supposed to learn in kindergarten is to replace your divots, in the broadest sense: if you use something, put it back when you're through with it. Perceivers are naturally more casual about that, and at a deeper level, may well have some passive-aggressive behavior going on that makes them want to rebel against people who try to enforce rules on them. Mature Perceivers have developed their Judging to a reasonable degree, and may be quite organized. Some, especially NP's, may be almost fanatical about getting things back "where they belong," because they know they won't be able to find them again otherwise.

Pot-Shots No 2475

LET'S MAKE IT DEFINITE:

I'LL SEE YOU WHEN I SEE YOU.

Ashleigh Brilliant

Perceivers are casual, unscheduled folks. Their calendars generally aren't as full in advance as comparable Judgers' are, but they still include lots of activity. It's just that it's more likely to be spur-of-the-moment, not planned so far ahead of time. Organizations that get their notices out late may still have a chance to attract Perceivers; but the Judgers' calendars are already booked up for that date. The Perceivers like to keep options open, to feel free to do whatever seems best to do when the time comes. They can and do learn to plan in advance; but it's not their natural preference. Perceivers usually aren't into controlling others— but they definitely don't like to *be* controlled themselves. An exception is in minor matters, where they're happy enough to have someone else make little decisions; they'll usually go along if there's no good reason not to.

Pot-Shots No 2729

I DON'T
KNOW
WHAT I'M
LOOKING FOR ~

THAT'S WHAT
MAKES
THE SEARCH
SO EXCITING !

Their open-ended attitude means Perceivers don't rely so much on long-range planning. (Long-range planning for Perceivers means, what am I going to do tomorrow?) For Perceivers, the hardest— and most important!— part of planning (aside from finding time and motivation) is deciding what *goals* to be working toward. Rather than specifically planning out their entire life, P's just live it, and are curious to find out how it all turns out.

Pot-Shots No 1437

ONE THING
YOU CAN
RELY ON

IS THAT
THERE WILL
ALWAYS BE
UNCERTAINTY.

As we discussed earlier, Perceivers recognize that we always have uncertainty, so they don't plan the way Judgers do. They may plan, but they assume the plan is tentative at best, and that the ultimate outcome may be very different from the original assumptions. They remain flexible, and proceed a bit like a sailboat, zig-zag tacking into the wind. They remain open to new facts and possibilities, and may be especially alert to take advantage of new opportunities, even though it may mean veering away from the original plan.

© Ashleigh Brilliant 1974   *Pot-Shots No 620*

THE BEST THING
ABOUT BEING TOO LATE

IS THAT THERE'S
NO MORE NEED
TO HURRY.

Winston Churchill, a famous Perceiving type, said, "The best way to be sure of catching a train is to miss the one before it." Perceivers tend to see time as an opportunity, and are focused on whatever they're doing, or whomever they're talking to at the moment. That means they may not remember (or plan accurately enough) to leave the present appointment in time to make the next one on time. Of course, some P's work very hard to be on time, especially in later life, because they recognize it's considered essential by Judgers.

Pot-Shots No 367

Perceivers and decisions. Yes, P's do make decisions, but they take longer. Sometimes they, in effect, *decide not to make a decision* (another way to decide). In that case, someone else may make the decision for them— probably a J with less information than the P had, but the J felt that was sufficient!

Summary— J & P

There are 2 things the brain does:
- Gets information (Perceiving)
- Decides what to do about it (Judging)

People prefer to operate in the *outer world* (i.e., when they Extravert) with one of two "Lifestyles:"

- **Perceiving**— getting more and more information, delaying decisions.
- **Judging**— deciding as quickly as possible, shutting off information flow as soon as it's feasible to decide and move on.

We all use *both* every day, but prefer one, and do that more often; so it gets better, more reliable, and we use it even more.

115

Specific contrasting traits, tendencies and behaviors tend to relate to each preference. Some may apply to you more than others. You may tend to be a Judger, but in some ways prefer to operate as a Perceiver, or vice versa. That's not unusual. Chapter 6 may help you determine your own preference.

Key Words— Judging & Perceiving	
Judging	**Perceiving**
Prepare in advance, avoid stress	Deadline pressure prompts best work
Organized, need orderliness, tidiness	Can deal comfortably with chaos
Dislike distractions, don't interrupt process	Interruptible, go with the flow
Plan/schedule to avoid stress; no surprises	Surprise me! Avoid routine
Great planners	Very flexible, can adapt and change
Plans are often thorough, detailed, step-by-step	Plans are often non-existent (would rather keep things open)
Value punctuality	Sometimes late due to distractions, plans changed
Comfortable once decisions made	Avoid decisions, uncomfortable once decided
Like to be in control (or at least be sure someone is!)	Like not to BE controlled!
Make judgments, decisions, cut off information	Take in information, avoid or postpone decisions
Speak in decisions, judgments	Speak in perceptions, non-judgments
Have lists, do them— in order	If have list, seldom follow it closely
Have expectations; want to make things fit plan	Have curiosity, interested to see how things turn out
Yes or no	Maybe (sometimes, "Yes, but...")
Negative: may be rigid, controlling, judgmental	Negative: may be wishy-washy, indecisive, plan poorly

*Adapted from "Key Words in Type," © 1988 William D. G. Murray

Which do you think you are— Judger or Perceiver?

Prefer Judging	**Undecided**	**Prefer Perceiving**
10	0	10

Chapter 5

The Four Temperaments

- **The NF Romantics**
- **The NT Scientists**
- **The SJ Conservators**
- **The SP Pragmatists**

OK, you've been through the 8 letters and you have a pretty good idea which 4 fit you best. But Type is more than just the four letters that are your preferences; when you combine two or more letters, you get something greater than the sum of the parts. For example, someone who is an iNtuitive(N) and also a Feeler (F) exhibits some "NF" traits that would not be predicted by either N or F. There are several ways the letters can be combined in pairs. Perhaps the most helpful, and probably best known, are the 4 "Temperaments" described by David Keirsey (and 2500 years ago, by Hippocrates). The old names were Melancholic, Sanguine, Choleric and Phlegmatic; Keirsey identifies these four classic Temperaments (or "humors," as they were called) with SJ, SP, NF, and NT combinations. We'll look at each in turn. First the NFs.

The NF Romantics

NFs will be creative **iNtuitives** and warm **Feelers**, of course; so they see possibilities for people. But they will also be the great romantics, a tendency not predicted by either letter alone.

© *Ashleigh Brilliant 1974*   *Pot-Shots No 599*

YOU'VE TOLD ME YOU LOVE ME, BUT THERE'S NO HARM IN REPEATING IT ENDLESSLY.

Ashleigh Brilliant

NFs are the romantics, in their daily relationships and their creations— they write romantic poetry and novels, tend to like schmaltzy, romantic music, and are most ready to "die for love." They are *not* like the Maine Yankee who, when his wife requested that he tell her he loved her and give her a kiss, said, "Will this take long?" NFs are usually unafraid of the "L" word, and tell each other (and want to *be* told) of their love on a frequent basis.

118

Pot-Shots No 283

I'M IN SEARCH
OF MYSELF ——

HAVE YOU SEEN ME ANYWHERE?

But NFs' great goal is discovering their "true self." "Who am I, really?" They are by nature the personal growth, human potential and "new age" folks, ever seeking, finding, and moving on to seek yet deeper insights into themselves and humankind. Their work areas and living rooms may be decorated with rainbows, unicorns, and beautiful nature scenes.

Pot-Shots No 1295

ALL MY LIFE, I'VE BEEN CHANGING —

WHEN WILL I
FINALLY BECOME
WHAT I'M REALLY
SUPPOSED TO BE?

Three of the Temperaments have goals—security (SJ), competence (NT), action (SP)— which seem understandable, even if you don't share them. But the NFs' goal of finding self doesn't sound like a real goal to the other Temperaments. "You mean your goal is to find out what your goal is? Then what's your goal after you find out what it is?"

UNFORTUNATELY,
THE CAUSES I SUPPORT
ARE USUALLY
UNPOPULAR ONES,

Ashleigh Brilliant

SUCH AS
THE CAUSE OF

HUMAN SURVIVAL.

© *Ashleigh Brilliant 1979*   *Pot-Shots No 1551*

Causes. Similarly, NFs will be great promoters of causes— often global in scope, such as environmentalism, conservation, world peace, and occasional ad hoc causes ("Free the Glutzberg Seven!") NFs are Feelers, and their causes will reflect their Feeling values— which may vary widely from Feeler to Feeler. Two NFs may strive with equal passion on opposite sides of the same issue. This is possible but less likely with Thinkers.

Perhaps it's best
to keep
some dreams
in my heart,

where they'll
always be
safe from
disappointment.

© *Ashleigh Brilliant 1988*   *Pot-Shots No 4770*

Idealists.   Maybe it goes with the causes, or the future hopeful possibilities iNtuitives focus on— but with a Feeling twist. NFs are our idealists. They hold themselves (and the rest of us) to the highest ideals. The League of Nations. The Peace Corps. And of course love and living happily ever after, where their romanticism merges with idealism and they may seek to merge with their partners. (Boundaries can be a real NF problem, but that's another whole book...)

WORDS
ARE VERY IMPORTANT
IN EXPRESSING FEELINGS

AND IN
CONCEALING
THEM.

　　　　　　　Pot-Shots No 1496

Wordsmiths. NFs are the great word people. The iNtuitive function plus their values and people focus (and if Walter Lowen* is right, their particular brain development) give them a powerful advantage in using the spoken and written word. Perhaps it's because they have a deep need to express those feelings. Many of the great orators, preachers, and creative artists of the pen have been NFs. Even presidents and political leaders: Lincoln and the Gettysburg address, Reagan the Great Communicator, Churchill and "blood, sweat and tears." Most of the poets and novelists and even a large percentage of our reporters have been and are NFs.

* Dichotomies of the Mind, by Walter Lowen, John Wiley & Sons, Inc, NY 1982

The NT Scientists

What good
is a
superior
mind,
without another
superior mind
to communicate with?

Pot-Shots No 687

NTs— those who prefer both i**N**tuition and **Thinking**— tend to do well scholastically, and may value learning for learning's sake. They are likely to develop intellectual or scientific interests, and enjoy others who share those interests. They generally appreciate others who have developed their own intellectual gifts, and may have little time for those who have not.

Competence is a major concern for NTs. They strive to be competent themselves, and expect others to be so as well. They set high standards or goals for themselves, and constantly inch their expectations upward as they achieve their targets. This applies to their own high goals, and to (lesser) standards they set for others.

Keirsey, in "Please Understand Me," says that NTs have a Promethean need for power over nature. That power can be translated as knowledge or understanding— the *ability* to control nature, i.e., knowledge or understanding— not necessarily actually *doing* it.

WHY AREN'T YOU
MORE GRATEFUL
WHEN I PROVE
HOW WRONG YOU'VE BEEN?

Ashleigh
Brilliant

Pot-Shots No 1407

NTs' intellectual prowess and Thinking orientation may lead them to be competitive, especially in arguments and intellectual matters. Winning proves their competence, which is what matters for them. Two NT's can have a fine time arguing; but if the NT is arguing with a Feeler, there may be misunderstanding when the Feeler feels attacked, and the NT can't imagine why.

I'M PERFECTLY WILLING TO BE JUDGED AND CRITICIZED,

Ashleigh Brilliant

BUT ONLY BY GOD AND HISTORY.

Pot-Shots No 655

NT's generally handle criticism well: they ignore it, unless they perceive it as coming from someone with significant intellectual or other credentials that makes their criticism worthy of consideration.   If it appears valid, they will pay attention, and make appropriate adjustments, not taking it personally as a Feeler is wont to do.   When dealing with an NT, you will do well to establish your credentials in their eyes first.

IT'S SOMETIMES
EASIER
TO INSIST ON
BEING WRONG
THAN IT IS
TO ADMIT
BEING IGNORANT.

Ashleigh Brilliant

© *Ashleigh Brilliant 1983*   *Pot-Shots No 2868*

NTs like to be right. (All Thinkers do, but especially NTs. It has to do with their need for competence.) They may argue strenuously and ingeniously to prove they are right, even (some might say especially) when they know they are wrong. Maybe that's why many lawyers are NTs; they must be able to carry on their side of an adversarial proceeding, be it for the plaintiff or defendant. It never hurts to allow anyone, but particularly an NT, a face-saving way out. Deep down most will know you're competent and to be respected, but will appreciate your not reducing their own feelings of self-esteem.

The SJ Conservators

I AM NOT RESPONSIBLE FOR THE WHOLE WORLD

BUT AM NOT SURE IF THE WORLD REALIZES THIS.

Pot-Shots No 1470

Sensing Judgers come at the world with their preferred deciding function: Thinking or Feeling. They Extravert it, so you hear decisions from them. They are the responsible types. Not the only responsible ones, but those who make a profession of it. They have an inner sense of responsibility that helps make them the pillars of society, playing leading roles in whatever organizations they may become involved with. If a situation arises where someone needs to take responsibility, SJs can usually be counted on to volunteer. *Noblesse oblige.*

YOU CAN CHANGE THE WORLD!

BUT, UNLESS YOU REALLY KNOW WHAT YOU'RE DOING, PLEASE DON'T!

© *Ashleigh Brilliant 1979*   *Pot-Shots No 1535*

SJ's are traditionalists who like to keep and preserve the best of the past and present— the status quo. They resist change, because they are dedicated to its opposite. They are thus a *stabilizing* force that prevents too-rapid changes due to an ill-advised new fad; and also a *brake* on the wheels of necessary and beneficial improvement. (Sometimes it's hard to tell which aspect is operating!)

By accepting you
as you are,
I do not
necessarily
abandon
all hope
of your
improving.

Pot-Shots No 1687

SJ's may like the status quo in most areas, but when it comes to wanting others for whom they feel responsible to shape up, SJ's can be counted on to work tirelessly toward that end. To paraphrase consultant Don Lowry, their marriage vows are to "love, honor, and change" the other person. This "shaping up," not surprisingly, usually means making the other more like the SJ— more attuned and obedient to the "rules" that govern the SJ's life. As Professor Henry Higgins put it in *My Fair Lady*, "Why can't a woman...be more like *me*?" Of course, we all have expectations of some sort in relationships, and want the other to conform to them. Perhaps the difference with SJ's is the idea of "rules" to be obeyed: the *shoulds* and *oughts* of life.

THE FUTURE SOUNDS WONDERFUL

BUT, CAN WE AFFORD IT ?

© *Ashleigh Brilliant 1980*   *Pot-Shots No 1800*

SJ's are the economic realists. As Sensors, they are focused in the present, not the future; and when visionary iNtuitors talk of magnificent future schemes, SJ's may bring them down to earth with fiscal facts and discipline.

As with every point we make in this book, it is true that not only SJ's tune in to financial reality; but it comes most naturally for them. I once attended an Association dinner at which we all had a choice of beef, chicken, or fish. The waitress went down the long table taking orders: Fish. Fish. Beef. Chicken. Chicken. As she came to the two SJ's in the group, each asked the prices before giving their order. No one else had. And, for whatever reasons, both SJ's ordered the item that cost 50¢ less than the others. SJ's tend to be conscious of prices and economic consequences. There are times we could all learn from their example.

IT'S EASY TO COME AND GO...

THE HARD THING IS TO REMAIN.

© Ashleigh Brilliant 1971   Pot-Shots No 251

It ties in with the "shoulds." Duty. Honor. Discipline. All those good Boy Scout values. SJ's tend to be strong on loyalty (ISFJ's the most so). Stick-to-it-ive-ness. That's not to say SJ's never succumb to temptation; all Types do. But SJ's may be a bit more likely to hang in there when the going gets tough, long after others have bailed out. (Whether this trait is an asset or a liability depends on the circumstances.)

Consistency is another part of this. SJ's value consistency. They usually don't value variety, and may resist change. In large organizations, consistency is normally valued, if not required. It makes the wheels run more smoothly in most operations, and SJ's are very conscious of this. (SJ's dominate most large organizations.)

The SP Pragmatists

I HOPE I GET
WHAT I WANT

Ashleigh Brilliant

Before
I stop
wanting it.

© *Ashleigh Brilliant 1975*   *Pot-Shots No 71*

Sensing Perceivers, the fourth Temperament style, come at the world with their Sensing function; they Extravert it. That's what you hear from them: present-moment perceptions, facts, observations, practical matter-of-fact statements. That's a "Type" observation.

Keirsey's Temperament approach goes a step further, and observes that SPs' strong, outer-world-focused Sensing gives them powerful *urges,* which they want to satisfy before the urge passes. That, in a sentence, is their major motivation— what makes SP's run. The Nike commercial says it: "Just *do* it!" The "it" may be climb the highest mountain (because it's there), go sky-diving, fix the car or other equipment, or go play touch football with the guys.

And play they do: SP's are often great athletes, because they are able to focus on the present when practicing, and repeat an action over and over until they get it perfected. But with all this diligence in practice, they believe in having fun more than any other Temperament. They tend to make work into fun. (SJ's tend to make fun into work.) Some of this SP tendency relates to satisfying those urges, *now!*

132

© *Ashleigh Brilliant 1974*   *Pot-Shots No 508*

SPs' propensity for quick action makes them good in a crisis: emergency rescue teams; crisis counselors; or in any job which is habitually crisis-like, such as pit-traders in the stock market. It is almost as if SPs do not really go through the usual 2-step process of perceiving something, and deciding what to do about it. Rather, in a crisis, it is as if their perception includes both the situation and the obvious necessary action they must take *instantly* to prevent disaster. They see something falling, and don't stop to think about how best to deal with that; they just dive and catch it! For many SP's, this is especially true with physical objects or equipment.

But there is something about the excitement of a crisis that makes SP's come alive, feel alive. If they don't have a crisis to deal with, some SP's may even create one, just to make things more interesting! (Of course, the other Types may not appreciate this.)

I AM A PERSON OF PRINCIPLE:

MY STRICTEST PRINCIPLE IS:

DO WHATEVER SEEMS BEST AT THE TIME.

Ashleigh Brilliant

Pot-Shots No 3079

SP's are the great pragmatists of life. *Do what works.* Never mind the theory. The pragmatic thing to do is often so obvious to an SP that it is hard for them to understand why anyone would want to do something else, just because the rules, laws, or standard operating procedures say otherwise. "The law is an ass" is a fitting SP quotation; at least, on those occasions where this is true, SP's are not afraid to say so. To paraphrase Bibfeldt, SPs believe in the theory of pragmatism— so long as it works!

Pot-Shots No 1388

AS SOON AS YOU FIRMLY DECIDE WHAT TO DO WITH YOUR FREEDOM,

Ashleigh Brilliant

YOU ARE NO LONGER FREE.

Here's an irony for anyone seeking freedom, which means (at least in a free country where freedom in general is taken for granted) chiefly iNtuitive types and Sensing Perceivers. In general, INTJs and INFJs are the Types most interested in freedom. As Js they can be controlling. NPs and SPs are more likely not to want to *be* controlled, than to want to control others. ENFJs at midlife can seek freedom, especially if they have until then given others control over their lives, i.e., done mostly what others expected of them. ENTJs can do the same thing, in a different way, in an organization which they serve; though they may control their area, they are controlled by the organization overall.

Sensing Judgers (SJs) may be in general least likely to be focused strongly on freedom as a value. They are more concerned with security, more hierarchical in nature and likely to believe in having everyone follow the rules, and when a problem arises they are likely to *limit* freedoms further with still more rules, which the Ns and SPs will ignore, especially if they seem inappropriate or unnecessarily restrictive. (How many people actually obey speed limits, especially 55 mph on Interstates in states that still retain that limit? 55 is honored more in the breach than the observance, because there is no widespread belief that 65 is unsafe, and there is no gas shortage any more; the original reasons for the law don't apply, and it now seems to exist chiefly to extract revenue randomly from the public. (There is of course also the effect of an individual's basic values, e.g., whether they are liberal or authoritarian, for example.)

ALWAYS FOLLOW ORDERS,

UNLESS THEY ARE OBVIOUSLY CRAZY OR ILLEGAL,

OR YOU HAVE A BETTER IDEA.

Ashleigh Brilliant

© *Ashleigh Brilliant 1988*   *Pot-Shots No 4474*

The military operates on two contradictory principles. The first, adhered to by the SJs (most of the military), is "always follow orders." Training, tradition, and tremendous fear of court martial support this view. The second principle is that stated in the Potshot® above, adhered to by iNtuitives and SPs who are there to make the system actually operate, especially in a crisis. Corporal Klinger in M.A.S.H., when his outfit needed 50 units of type A positive blood, would get on the radiophone and get it by trading six canned hams and three truck tires. Totally illegal, of course, but the crazy (legal) alternative was to obey the rules, go through channels, and let men bleed to death. If time and enemy fire permitted, paperwork would be created after the fact to legalize the transactions, of course.

Summary—
The 4 Temperaments

There are several ways we can group sets of 4 Types that have 2 letters in common, e.g., all those with Extraversion and Feeling (EF) will be especially warm "people people." Perhaps the most helpful approach is David Keirsey's "4 Temperaments," which he identifies with Hippocrates' 4 Temperaments ("humors").

136

These are simpler, easy to identify; 4 Temperaments are easier to learn than 16 Types. The 4 Temperaments are:

- **The NF Romantics** (creative iNtuition + warm Feeling)
- **The NT Scientists** (creative iNtuition + logical Thinking)
- **The SJ Conservators** (practical Sensing + organized Judging)
- **The SP Pragmatists** (practical Sensing + flexible Perceiving)

The combining of two letters gives a richer way to look at people, for an NF has other characteristics beyond what would be predicted from simply N plus F. To summarize briefly:

Key Words— 4 Temperaments*	
NF Romantics idealists causes poetry, novels schmaltzy music search for self wordsmiths goal: integrity self-actualization rainbows & unicorns	**NT Scientists** learning for learning's sake intellectual interests, scholarship competence power over nature want to be right (even in small matters) require you to have credentials enjoy good argument, especially theoretical argument what's in it for me?
SJ Conservators responsible traditionalists resist change shoulds and oughts economic duty honor discipline consistency noblesse oblige	**SP Pragmatists** feel urge, want to satisfy it— now good in crisis whatever works risk-takers fun hands-on tools, equipment crafts what's in it for me?

*Adapted from "Key Words in Type," © 1988 William D. G. Murray

Which Temperament seems to fit you best? That probably has two letters of your Type in it, and indicates the kind of people you will find it easiest to communicate with. Rank them 1-2-3-4. Which seems to fit you least? You may have to work especially hard to communicate with people of this Temperament. Nonetheless, we all use all four Temperaments at one time or another.

Chapter 6

What Type Are You?

It's important to *know* your Type. If you don't know already, or aren't sure (popular ideas of Extraversion and Introversion may be misleading), the checklist on the next few pages will help you figure it out.

If you *do* know your Type, you may find the Checklist a useful review of key aspects of each of the 8 letters of Type. (If you're a Type expert, you may want to skip to Chapter 7 and read your own Type description, and those of significant others.)

Your Type is described by 4 letters— your preferences on each of 4 choices:

Attitude or Energy Direction	Perceiving Function	Deciding Function	Attitude or Lifestyle
E	S	T	J
I	N	F	P

In the first four chapters you've read about the 4 pairs of choices— E-I, S-N, T-F, and J-P— and perhaps tentatively decided which of each pair you prefer and use most often, and which you use less and find less dependable. With every pair of preferences, *we all use both,* every day— *but prefer one.*

So you have identified 4 letters that are "you." Maybe E,N,F,and P, (ENFP) or I,S,T and J (ISTJ); or some other combination. We call those 4 letters your "Type," assuming that you've

138

correctly identified yourself from the way we've described the preferences.

And in Chapter 5 you've read about the 4 Temperaments— NF, NT, SJ, and SP—and decided which is most like you, and which least like you. In most cases, the *two letters* of your Temperament will *both* be in your 4-letter Type.

The following Type Checklist is a quick and easy way to review your choices and check your first impression. It is NOT a heavily researched instrument, and is intended *only* to give you a general idea of your probable preferences.

Now go through the Checklist. Starting with Extravert & Introvert, choose which of each two choices (*the one on the left-hand page or the right-hand page*) is *more* like you, the way you really are— not the way you would *like* to be. Most people do both— but prefer one. Total the checks on each page, and compare the scores for each opposing preference; if the result is clearly one-sided, that's an indication that you clearly *prefer* that function or attitude over its opposite. Consider this result your "probable Type," at least while you read this book. If the scores are close on a given pair, you may want to explore both possibilities further; don't decide that you "are" either one too quickly. Read the more detailed Type description of your probable Type(s) in Chapter 7. Ask friends how they see you. You may then want to pursue the matter with a professional or join a local Type organization. We can put you in touch with Type organizations near you [Type & Temperament, Inc., Box 200, Gladwyne, PA 19035-0200 USA Tel. (610) 527-2330].

You may also want to try taking the Checklist for your spouse or someone else close to you, as you think they would answer. Then have them do the same for you, and compare how you see yourself, to how you are seen by the other person. This can be done by the two of you, or with a Type-oriented counselor or pastor. (If you find this discussion difficult or are having problems in the relationship, consult a counselor familiar with Type; many are not yet fully familiar with Type.)

If You Are...   Extravert:

Think externally, out loud ☐
Like people around, are outgoing ☐
Like involvement with people ☐
Like action/ variety ☐
Are fast, dislike complications ☐
Decide more quickly, have more immediate reactions ☐
Good greeter ☐
Communicate freely ☐
Easy warmth with many ☐
May not mind phone interruption ☐
Interested in results of job ☐
Impatient with long, slow jobs ☐
People always know where you stand ☐
Tend to spread ideas and use energy ☐
Broad interests— generalist ☐
Focus energy outward onto people and things ☐
Need public forum to sort things out ☐
Energized by putting energy out ☐
Like action, seek it out, initiate it ☐
Act first, reflect later (Active) ☐
Trial & error approach; error not failure but feedback ☐
Try it out before you spend energy thinking about it ☐
Require less certainty before acting ☐
Don't understand life 'til you have lived it ☐
May appear shallow to Introvert ☐

Total Extravert items checked ____

Introvert:

☐ Think internally
☐ Work alone well, prefer quiet
☐ Like detachment
☐ Need quiet "alone" time
☐ More careful with details
☐ Slower deciding, think it through carefully
☐ Trouble with names and faces
☐ Communicate less freely
☐ Depth of communication with a few
☐ Dislike phone interruption
☐ Interested in *idea* behind the job
☐ Can handle one project uninterruptedly
☐ People may not know where you stand
☐ Tend to consolidate and conserve energy
☐ Depth of interest— specialist
☐ Focus energy inward, into world of ideas/concepts
☐ Need time alone to sort things out
☐ Energized by taking in energy/ideas
☐ Like contemplation, find it stimulating
☐ Think first, act later (Reflective)
☐ Test ideas & shape them
☐ Try out internally before you speak or act on it
☐ Require more certainty before acting
☐ Won't live life 'til you understand it
☐ May appear withdrawn to Extravert

_____ **Total Introvert items checked**

Senser:

Strong capacity in the 5 senses ☐
In touch with reality— the *facts* ☐
Interest in here & now, the present, what *is* ☐
Observant ☐
Rely on data, strong sense of reality ☐
Use what you have learned ☐
Enjoy ☐
Hardheaded realist ☐
Practical ☐
Happy with the status quo ☐
Photographic perception ☐
See trees, specifics, notice details (veins on leaf) ☐
Solution must be workable ☐
Enjoyment now ☐
Simplicity ☐
Thorough ☐
Linear, sequential, step-by-step ☐
More tolerant of routine ☐
Read & follow directions ☐
Appreciate little things of life ☐
Want to do things better ☐
Consistency/countable-on ☐
Slower, but precise ☐
Local ☐
Won't waste time on the impossible ☐
Perspiration ☐
Getter-doner ☐
Concrete ☐
See reality ☐
Definition, fact ☐
You know, & you know how you know ☐
Negatives: May be too set in ways ☐
May be dull, unimaginative, miss opportunities ☐

Total Senser items checked _____

iNtuitive:

- [ ] Strong "6th sense," hunches reliable, powerful
- [ ] In touch with *possibilities, inferences*
- [ ] Interest in the future, imagining what *could* be
- [ ] Imaginative, new ideas
- [ ] Data as starting point, mental leaps to new ideas
- [ ] Learn something else new
- [ ] Anticipate
- [ ] Ability to read between the lines
- [ ] Creative
- [ ] Want growth, change, improvement
- [ ] Impressionistic perception
- [ ] See the forest, the big picture (don't notice leaves)
- [ ] Solution must allow growth/change
- [ ] Future enjoyment
- [ ] Complexity
- [ ] Innovative
- [ ] Random, start in middle, jump around
- [ ] Work in bursts of energy
- [ ] Follow hunch (If all else fails, may read directions)
- [ ] Don't notice little things, aim at future
- [ ] Want to do things differently
- [ ] Change/variety
- [ ] Faster, but approximate
- [ ] Global
- [ ] May attempt the impossible (may sometimes succeed)
- [ ] Inspiration
- [ ] Thinker-upper
- [ ] Abstract
- [ ] See meanings
- [ ] Metaphor, simile
- [ ] You know, but not sure how; you just know
- [ ] Negatives: May fail to enjoy the present
- [ ] May be unrealistic, follow impossible dreams

_____ **Total iNtuitive items checked**

Thinker:

Decision based on, "Is it logical?" ☐
Is it the truth? ☐
Objective, logical criteria ☐
Impersonal criteria ☐
Great planner ☐
Want justice ☐
Able to reprimand/fire people ☐
Firm-minded ☐
Use few words ☐
Hold to policy ☐
Need to be treated fairly ☐
Time frame is linear, past-present-future ☐
Priority is the task at hand ☐
Good at finding flaws ☐
If job well done, may say nothing ☐
May be too critical ☐
Relatively unaffected by dissension ☐
Like to be right (even in little things) ☐
Analytical ☐
Skeptical ☐
Message is more important than how you say it ☐

May hurt others' feelings unintentionally ☐

Negatives: *May* appear cold, unfeeling, aloof ☐

Total Thinker items checked ____

Feeler:

☐ Decision based on how it will affect the people
☐ Is it right or wrong, good or bad?
☐ Subjective criteria, depends on circumstances
☐ Personal criteria, value system
☐ Great "people person"
☐ Want harmony
☐ Dislike any unpleasantness
☐ Personal warmth
☐ Talker
☐ Make exceptions as needed
☐ Need to be appreciated & praised
☐ Time frame focuses on the past, may try to recreate it
☐ Priority is the relationship(s) involved
☐ Good appreciator, find what's OK
☐ Need and give constant feedback, especially praise
☐ May stifle or ignore needed criticism
☐ Tend to take everything personally
☐ Like to please people (even in little things)
☐ Sympathetic
☐ Trusting
☐ How something is said (body language, tone, expression, pleasantness) is vital
☐ *May* be intolerant of people who unintentionally hurt others' feelings
☐ Negatives: *May* appear illogical, disorganized, over-emotional

_____ **Total Feeler items checked**

145

Judger:

Like making decisions ☐
Like to get things decided quickly ☐
May decide too fast ☐
Great planner ☐
Hate surprises ☐
Want to control & regulate things (your life, others') ☐
Organize things, require order and organization ☐
Goal-oriented ☐
Batch processor, finish one thing before ☐
starting next; a start-to-finish systematic approach
Dislike interruptions ☐
May not notice new things that need doing ☐
Once decided, tend to be satisfied ☐
Value punctuality ☐
See time as limited resource to be allocated ☐
Make definite final statements ☐
Speak in decisions, judgments ☐
Anxious when decision not reached yet ☐
Tend to hear answers as decisions when not yet decided ☐
Want to know only the essentials ☐
Negatives: *May* adjust poorly to change ☐
May be rigid, controlling, judgmental ☐

Total Judger items checked _____

Your scores:

1. Attitude: E_____ or   I_____   Difference_____
2. Function   S_____ or   N_____   Difference_____
3. Function   T_____ or   F_____   Difference_____
4. Lifestyle   J_____ or   P_____   Difference_____

List below the larger item from each line above:

1. _____ 2. _____ 3. _____ 4. _____ This is your 4-letter Type preference (e.g., E-N-T-J), based on this tentative information. See comments on how to confirm or modify it as appropriate to determine your "True Type."

Perceiver:

- [ ] Like taking in information
- [ ] Like to get more information, defer decision
- [ ] May decide too slowly
- [ ] Very flexible, can adapt and change
- [ ] Don't mind surprises, may enjoy them
- [ ] Want to understand things, see how life turns out
- [ ] Can work without organizing first, can handle chaos
- [ ] Process-oriented
- [ ] Parallel processor, several things going on at once, work on all
- [ ] Interruptible, shift gears easily
- [ ] May postpone unpleasant jobs, procrastinate
- [ ] Tend to be curious, welcome new info
- [ ] May be late because plans changed
- [ ] See time as opportunity
- [ ] Offer options: "On the one hand......"
- [ ] Speak in perceptions, non-judgments
- [ ] Anxious after reaching decision
- [ ] Tend to hear answers as *not* decided, when they *were*
- [ ] Want to know all about it
- [ ] Negatives: *May* start too many projects, not finish any
- [ ] *May* be wishy-washy, indecisive, plan poorly

_____ **Total Perceiver items checked**

Note: As stated, S & N are *perceiving* functions, T & F are *judging* functions. *Everyone uses all 4 functions, though only the 2 preferred show up in your Type.*

We have a 1-2-3-4 order of preference for the 4 functions, which depends on our Type. We tend to develop all 4 in order over the years, even though only two of the four show in our 4-letter Type. The #1, most-preferred function is often called the Dominant; #2 is the Auxiliary, #3 the Tertiary, and the 4th is called variously the Inferior, least-preferred, or "shadow function." The 4th is largely *unconscious,* and is usually not much developed until midlife. The Type descriptions in Chapter 7 describe these for each Type. They are summarized in a Table in the Energy Direction appendix.

Letters and Symbols in the 16 Type Descriptions in Chapter 7:

The 8 Letters— E,I,S,N,T,F,J,and P represent the 8 letters of Type decribed in Chapters 1 through 4.

Functions— The 2 middle letters in your 4-letter Type indicate the way you prefer to *get information* (2nd letter— either S or N) and the way you prefer to *make decisions* (3rd letter, either T or F).

Though we all use each function in each direction— Introvertedly and Extravertedly— *we also have a preference in the direction* we usually use each function. There is a regular, generally predictable pattern for each Type. Thus, an ENFP uses N Extravertedly (which we designate as "Ne") and F Introvertedly (which we designate as "Fi"), and T Extravertedly (Te) and S Introvertedly (Si).

Se— Extraverted Sensing	**Te**— Extraverted Thinking
Si— Introverted Sensing	**Ti**— Introverted Thinking
Ne— Extraverted iNtuition	**Fe**— Extraverted Feeling
Ni— Introverted iNtuition	**Fi**— Introverted Feeling

2-Letter Combinations, such as NF, NT, SJ, and SP (the "4 Temperaments") are also used in the Type descriptions. It is possible to get special insights from combining other pairs, such as the "Attitude/Lifestyle Pairs," E--P, I--P, E--J, and E--P, which are often easily identifiable by observation of an individual. Where appropriate, we have used various pairs to flesh out the Type Descriptions.

Determining Your "True Type"

Your "True Type" represents your natural preferences; everyone has a True Type. We were probably born with it, or at least locked into it very early. One way to find out what it is, is to take a Type indicator, such as the Checklist on the preceding pages. There is a tendency to assume that this result is your True Type. This is not a safe bet, especially if you have one or more close scores. With our Type Checklist, or the Myers-Briggs Type Indicator®*, or any other Indicator, there is a good chance that one or more of your letters will be misidentified. Use the results as a starting point, or Probable Type. Next read the Type Description for this Type, and also for the other(s) that would apply if you in fact preferred the *other* letter in each close score. If you score ENFP, but are close on J and P, read ENFP and then ENFJ descriptions. (If you have two close scores, you will have 4 descriptions to read.) Have someone who knows you well read the description(s) also and get their input.

Now review the 4 Temperaments, and see which is the best fit. This can often give a powerful clue when your Type score is unclear, e.g., if you are either ISFP or INFP, read the SP vs NF Temperaments in Chapter 5, or in a book such as Keirsey & Bates' "Please Understand Me."

Also consider carefully which of the 4 functions is your *strongest*, then which is the *toughest* for you to deal with. Sometimes it's easier to identify your *least*-developed (4th) function than it is to be sure about your Dominant or strongest.

You may benefit from reading other books on Type, and other Type descriptions; or perhaps you'll want to get in touch with a Type professional to work on this further. [For names of Type experts in your area, call Type & Temperament, Inc, at 1-(800) IHS-TYPE.]

* Myers-Briggs Type Indicator® and MBTI® are registered copyrights of Consulting Psychologists Press.

THE SECRET OF SELLING YOURSELF

IS
TO HAVE
A PRODUCT
YOU TRULY
BELIEVE IN.

Ashleigh Brilliant

The first benefit of Type is *self-esteem*. Few things you can learn in so short a time are as powerful as discovering for yourself such great depth of information about who you truly are, your strengths and weaknesses, and the recognition that you're perfectly OK. There are lots of others very much like you, though they may or may not be heavily represented in your group of acquaintances. Some Types are "1% Types, " that is, only about 1% of the U.S. population is that Type. Some are 12% (percentages are approximate—see Type Table opposite). Knowing your strengths can help you function better in whatever you do— and help you choose a career that makes the most of your natural advantages— while letting you develop your less-preferred side safely, without messing up your life. (See Chapter 8.)

The second benefit of Type is *communication*— understanding the other guy, so that you can communicate better (in both directions— speaking so she "hears" you, and listening so you understand and appreciate her). For example, if you recognize that someone is an Introvert, and **you're an Extravert who speaks loudly,** you'll communicate better if you talk more quietly. Try it. It really helps.

Chapter 7

The 16 Type Descriptions

ISTJ	ISFJ	INFJ	INTJ
6%	6%	1%	1%
pg 152	pg 168	pg184	pg 200
ISTP	ISFP	INFP	INTP
6%	6%	1%	1%
pg 156	pg 172	pg 188	pg 204
ESTP	ESFP	ENFP	ENTP
12%	12%	5%	5%
pg 160	pg 176	pg 192	pg 208
ESTJ	ESFJ	ENFJ	ENTJ
12%	12%	5%	5%
pg 164	pg 180	pg 196	pg 212

ISTJ—Introverted Senser with Extraverted Thinking

Overview— ISTJs are quiet, practical, logical and organized. The most responsible of the 16 Types, they learn what they need to learn to do what must be done. Hard workers, many rise to managerial positions through their loyalty and dependability, practical common-sense approach, and tough-minded decisiveness. As Dominant Sensers their time focus is the here-and-now present.

ISTJs are Introverted, Sensing, Thinking and Judging— Introverted Sensers, who when they deal with the outer world prefer to use their logical Thinking function.

I— Introverted ISTJs are generally quiet, though they will speak up when something needs to be said. In a music group of four Introverts, the ISTJ became the primary spokesperson at performances, because it had to be done.

Si— **Sensing** is the ISTJ's **Dominant** or most preferred function, but it is **Introverted** and not visible to others. It stores incredibly detailed photographic images of whatever the ISTJ's senses have experienced, and keeps these experiences in random access memory, for guidance when a similar situation arises. They see and remember detail that iNtuitives do not notice, and relate it to what is meaningful to them.

Powerful Sensing provides constant input on the real world— what is happening here, now. This gives ISTJs a practical, commonsense approach that is pragmatic and effective— but tends to favor the tried and true, and resist the new.

Te— ISTJs come at the world with their **Extraverted Thinking** judgment, their **Auxiliary** or second-best function. This is heard as logical critiquing, often negative judgments as to why something won't work, or hasn't been done before. They can be quite good at keeping their cool, but may appear too cool and unemotional to Feelers who are looking for a warmer contact. As ISTJs use their Thinking to deal with the world, it can become very well developed, and they may appear to be Extraverts, and take on positions of leadership requiring considerable Extraversion (but as true Introverts, they will still need to shut down to charge their batteries).

J— As decisive **Judgers**, ISTJs are planful and detailed, neat and orderly. If something has been moved, they will spot it. They naturally schedule things, see schedules as commitments, and assume others do the same. (In dealing with ISTJs it's especially important to be on time, keep all commitments, due dates, etc. Everyone appreciates it; ISTJs expect it.)

Fi— Feeling judgment, the ISTJ's **3rd-preferred** function, is **Introverted** and not easily accessible. It may take some time to decide how they feel about something, when a Feeling judgment is required. They may give the impression of being a "Stonewall" both in expression and demeanor. In very emotional situations they may keep so calm as to be frightening; their Thinking function is in command and the Feeling side can't come out until allowed. Later, alone in private, they may access the Feeling side; but rarely is it verbalized in public.

"Shadow Side" 4th Function — Ne— iNtuition is the least-developed side of an ISTJ, but it tends to be **Extraverted** when it is used. It may show up as a wry, quirky sense of humor. It is also the part that looks at the future, and when it does, it tends to see few possibilities, all bad. ISTJs can project a "doom and gloom" view of things, especially when stressed or depressed. (The antidote is often simply to get them using their preferred Introverted Sensing again; go dig in the garden, or organize a file or two.) They may overinvest in insurance against extremely unlikely events.

SJ— By Temperament ISTJs are "SJs," that combination of practicality and organization that gets so much done. They are the super-responsible folks who live by the rules, regulations, Standard Operating Procedures, Guidelines— the *shoulds* and *oughts* of society. ISTJs are prominent among those making and enforcing the laws, and they believe you should obey them, too. (An ISTJ going exactly 55 mph in the fast lane was almost run off the road by a trucker who wished to go 56 or more but couldn't.)

ISTJs are "economic Types." They are conscious of, aware of the value of, and good at handling money in all its forms. They are aware of prices, and consider price and value to be important in their purchases.

ST— The ISTJ's preferred functions, Sensing and Thinking, give them a special slant on life: practical and logical, they abound in business, where such traits are particularly helpful. It gives them realism needed to understand the present practical problems, and objectivity to deal with the here and now, decisively and in an orderly way. They can do the tough stuff— disciplining and firing— because it is necessary. They deal with numbers, accounting and analysis well— practical facts, handled logically.

IJ— As Introverted Judgers, ISTJs are always reorganizing the content of their mental data banks. They go inside their incredible unstructured memory banks for data to solve problems. They think inductively, using the data to define the problem and the solution.

TJ— ISTJs are one of the four "TJ" Types that rule the world— the four "sharp corners" of the Type table. The combination of logical processing(T) and a desire to get decisions made promptly, to plan and schedule things in detail and follow through on them (J), can make for an efficient organization.

ISTJ Life Themes— Responsibility, duty, doing what one ought to do, is a major life theme for ISTJs. Economic concerns and investments, frugality, preparing for a (disastrous, they fear) future, are part of their style. The fable of the (ISTJ) ant and the grasshopper (a Perceiving Type insect who does not plan or save well) shows that we have long recognized ISTJs, even before Type was known. Note that the ant, though not happy about it, does care for the grasshopper when winter catches him unprepared. ISTJs are civic heroes, pillars of every community, helping those whom life or absence of self-discipline has dealt with badly, conserving the treasuries and directing the efforts of all manner of organizations.

How to Spot ISTJs— ISTJs, 6% of the population, are often found in management positions in large organizations, and in engineering, scientific, or accounting occupations. They are active in civic affairs. Seriousness is usually a hallmark (with the occasional quirky humor noted). President Nixon, a probable ISTJ, said he didn't trust people who smiled much. ISTJs' own smiles, when they occur, are often archaic, as if they had not practiced enough to get it quite right. (This is more true of male ISTJs.) ISTJs are quiet, businesslike, not usually given to chit-chat. You hear logical judgments from them. Practical, economic, conservative in dress and views, they know bargains and what things cost. ISTJs can be quite private, and hard to get close to— though it may be worth the effort.

Gender Differences— There can be significant sex/gender differences among ISTJs. The male of the species is more likely to be a no-nonsense, cool, unsmiling type (though some are quite congenial and aggressively friendly, they are the exception). Males may act "macho." At work some can be seemingly devoid of emotion, especially if the job requires it, e.g., prison guards. Later in life they may develop the softer iNtuitive Feeler that is part of their less-conscious side.

ISTJ women are obviously walking a tough path if they

behave like the macho man— but in practice they usually are socialized to "be more feminine," i.e., to develop their softer Feeling side. But they retain the strength of character, practicality, logic, and organization that makes them excellent homemakers (as a career or in addition to another career). One study shows ISTJ women on average the easiest to be married to— though there is no "easy" relationship. When a male expects the female to carry the Feeling side in a relationship, the ISTJ woman is being asked to do it with her third-best function, which is Introverted and not easily accessible. In this situation, outside counseling may be helpful.

ISTJ Key Words

modest	routine	conserve	predictable
privacy	simplicity	consistent	realist
quiet	specifics	durability	reliable
concrete	analytical	duty	responsibility
detailed	impersonal	formality	rules
doom and gloom	justice	hard working	S.O.P.s
facts	logical	hierarchical	serious
here-and-now	systematic	legalistic	shoulds
literal	decisive	loyalty	stability
matter-of-fact	follow-through	obligations	super-dependable
no-nonsense	neat	perseverance	traditional
one-at-a-time	organized	pessimist	thorough
practical	scheduled	pillars	
realistic	timely	precise	

`TP— Introverted Thinker with Extraverted Sensing

STPs are quiet but action-oriented, extremely practi-
skilled in logical analysis— but may not let you
They show you their propensity for detailed
fact. knowledge, their flexibility, their crisis orientation. They are
about 6% of population.

As Dominant Thinkers their time focus is a logical linear
past-to-present-to-future flow. They basically live today, using the
experience of the past to plan for the future.

ISTPs are Introverted, Sensing, Thinking and Perceiving—
logical Introverted Thinkers, who when they deal with the outer
world prefer to use their practical Sensing function.

I— ISTPs keep their own counsel, working on their own problems
in their minds with little evidence to show the world what's really
going on. With their casual demeanor, people are often surprised at
the depth of their thinking when they choose to reveal a bit. They
develop their own principles, an understanding of what makes the
world work, and operate on that basis, right or wrong. It takes a great
deal to get them to change their underlying worldview, though they
will listen to other arguments (up to a point).

They may be shy children, or in the right situation— most
likely sports—may run with a group of buddies.

Se— Their **Extraverted Sensing** is a finely tuned instrument that
feeds them sense impressions in exquisite detail. Some can listen to
a car engine and tell which valve is sticking. This Sensing, their
second-best or **Auxiliary** function, is their primary communication
with the outer world. It provides them (and you) with the facts about
a situation, object or person. Their Thinking analyzes and incorpo-
rates these into their internal Operating Procedures— though you
may never see this result.

Sensing makes them eminently practical. They operate on
the facts, and have little motivation to do or learn things that have no
practical application. Learning for learning's sake is not for the
ISTP, as it would be for the INTP. Ditto with art for art's sake,
though they may be artistic. ISTPs have a sense of the essence of line
and form that stands them in good stead if they become cartoonists,
masters of caricature.

Ti— ISTPs' **Dominant Thinking** is **Introverted**, giving them
doubly strong tendencies to be detached from the outer world
situation. Good at finding the flaws, their often abrupt manner can

be upsetting to Feelers. A major indicator of ISTP growth is their ability to deal successfully with Feelers, as they learn to praise first, then offer their criticism.

P— Casual **Perceptive** types, ISTPs are laid-back and don't need to make things happen their way, so much as to understand how and why they are happening, and perhaps adjust accordingly. They prefer to wait and see rather than leap in with a decision as an E-J Type might (although in a crisis they may spontaneously "do the necessary" based on their powerful background knowledge of facts and keen observations).

Ni— Introverted iNtuition is an ISTP's **3rd function**, key input that outlines options for analysis and decision-making by the Dominant Thinking. From age 18 to midlife it grows in impact, but is rarely seen by others.

"Shadow Side" 4th Function — Fe – Extraverted Feeling is the ISTP's fourth or "shadow function." Least conscious, it can be the source of much joy and pain for the ISTP. Because it is Extraverted, it shows—at least occasionally. It may give the ISTP much warmth, and some may seem to be Extraverts. Extraverted Feeling, however, may be more fixed on the other, new person than on those nearest and dearest, who may sometimes feel taken for granted.

Sometimes the ISTP is criticized more for *omitting* the little Feeling niceties that do not come naturally, more so than for overt criticism, anger, or actual negative expression of emotion. Learning the generally accepted social skills can go a long way toward helping an ISTP's career and general social life. Nonetheless, they can be loyal friends in need!

ISTPs are clear on their logical principles; they are fuzzy on Feeling values, which may make little sense (logically). In later life they may come to develop this side, but it seldom comes easily. They may be uncomfortable with people and try to suppress their own emotional reactions. As with all Dominant Thinkers, they can be subject to losing control and expressing a feeling— anger— with great force; then calming down, and resolving to be even more diligent in suppressing. Unfortunately, this tactic does not work indefinitely, and the short term control can lead to long term disaster.

There can be a tendency, especially at midlife, as this Feeling function is developing, to fixate or project onto another person, who becomes a love object and is seen as perfection itself. Often this person really represents a part of the ISTP that needs to be developed. If this can be understood as the real purpose, the situation can be richly rewarding, without disastrous effects on the ISTP's and others' lives.

SP— Though Introverts, ISTPs also have the SP Temperament, and may tend to like some action and excitement. This can combine with their common interest in things mechanical, where their Extraverted Sensing gives them the "feel" of the equipment— e.g., auto racers, motorcyclists, or carrier pilots. At some level, ISTPs may have great digital dexterity and very sensitive fingertips, which gives them an advantage as sculptors and woodworkers, for example. Besides artisans, they may be consummate performers— in sports, dancing or music— who can go over a routine tirelessly until it is perfected to world-class level. They may have difficulties in school, few of which teach them in the mode in which they learn best.

Like iNtuitives, SPs have a keen sense of personal independence (though often with more urge toward comraderie than Ns) and a tendency to proceed without directions ("if all else fails, read the directions"). They are likely to promote similar independence in their own children, not be controllers.

ST— The **Sensing-Thinking** combination gives ISTPs a comfort with numbers, math, accounting, and practical business sense. They can be extremely good with finances— or they may exhibit a one-day-at-a-time approach that SJs would label irresponsible. They might go either way on this.

IP— As IPs, they are "closet Js," that is they operate as casual Perceivers, but their Dominant function is actually a deciding one, and they like to get things decided, though they take their time and want to fit things perfectly into their worldview.

TP— **Thinking Perceivers** are casual folks who decide things with logic, but show the world their warmer Feeling function, which can mislead those who take it at face value and expect a people-oriented values-based Feeling decision— only to get a cold objective Thinking decision that may step on some toes. You can't always tell what the judge is thinking!

ISTP Life Themes— ISTPs need to feel the impulse to act, and to satisfy it now by acting. When they don't have an impulse, motivation is reduced, and they have to work at it.

Often there is a hands-on nature to much that ISTPs do, from micro (manual dexterity) to macro (running huge equipment), plus sports and other areas. ISTPs don't usually like to sit still enough to stay in sedentary jobs. Their management style is hands-on, also, often MBWA (Management By Walking Around), though not so socially as an Extravert might be.

As Dominant Introverted Thinkers, they may seem aloof, cool, not much caring to be involved. They may seem blunt to Feelers, and hurt feelings unintentionally, until they learn to avoid this (if they care to; some may not, seeing it, not without some justification, as usually the Feeler's problem).

How to Spot ISTPs— ISTPs can be hard for others to identify. As Introverts, they display the other three letters less often and less obviously. Also, they may run hot and cool, so it's hard to tell which is the "real" person. Look for a quiet but action-oriented person, tending to be somewhat physical at times— but otherwise relaxed, less active and even seemingly lazy when not engaged in activities of personal interest. The SP Temperament is likely to show as you get to know an ISTP, along with the Dominant Thinking (logical decisions).

Gender Differences— There are major sex/gender differences with ISTPs, as with all Dominant Thinkers. Male ISTPs tend to be "macho" and enjoy rough, exciting, perhaps risky, stereotypically male activities. So do some ISTP females, but society tends to frown on this and tries to steer them into more subdued versions— though increasingly women are finding careers in more physical occupations. Besides being an SP, the female ISTP has the classic "female Thinker" problem in a world that expects women to be Feelers. Ultimately this can be a career advantage because they are socialized as Feelers. Thus they have more of the strengths of both sides; male ISTPs have a harder time developing their Feeling side at midlife.

ISTP Key Words

quiet	practical	curious	experiential
reserved	realism	flexible	freedom
solitude	specific	action	hands-on
applications	tangible	adventure	individualistic
concrete	utilitarian	artisan	perseverance
data	analytical	bold	physical
facts	impersonal	crisis	risk-taker
observant	logical	excitement	spontaneous

ESTP—Extraverted Sensing with Introverted Thinking

Overview— ESTPs are energetic, charming, outgoing and enthusiastic risk-takers, spontaneous and adaptable, action-oriented. As Dominant Sensers their time focus is right now.

ESTPs are Extraverted, Sensing, Thinking and Perceiving. Or more accurately, Extraverted Sensers, who when they make important decisions prefer to use their logical analytical Thinking function, for which they need quiet introverted time.

E— ESTPs receive their key inputs from the outer world of people and things, as their five senses provide them with a continuing stream of data, to which they are remarkably well attuned. They learn through experience, through action— which they are constantly engaged in, since they are doers more than contemplaters. "Just do it" is the advertising slogan that sums up their style; they are masters of the spontaneous action, trial-and-error learning, prompted and guided and constantly adjusted by their powerful senses. They are supremely comfortable and at home in the environment. ESTPs are about 12% of the U.S. population.

Se— **Extraverted Sensing** is their longest and strongest suit, the **Dominant,** and it calls the shots for them in most of what they do. It keeps them advised on the state of the real world at all times; no one is better connected to reality. They are supreme realists, practical, concrete, fact-based and matter-of fact. They are great data-handlers, be it numbers, facts, or physical materials. They are tuned to the physical, to sports, exercise, and hands-on operation of all types of equipment.

Ti— ESTPs **Introvert** their **Auxiliary** function, **Thinking.** They focus more on things than people, though they are especially conscious of subtle details of others' appearance, physical and mental state. This makes them very good negotiators, and keeps them objective, not caught up in the cause behind the negotiation. They are great pragmatists, not idealists. "Whatever works" is their motto.

P— Flexible and spontaneous **Perceivers,** ESTPs prefer to postpone decisions, or rather to make little "non-decisions" as they go along, simply "doing the necessary" as the situation demands. Often their decisions seem to be made by perception rather than judgment, instantly, particularly in a crisis. They are good broken field runners, constantly adjusting to the shifting of the opposition— literally, in football, or analogously in many other situations in life. They in fact like to play, and find ways to make work play whenever they can.

Fe— Feeling, the **3rd function,** is **Extraverted** for ESTPs, and they are natural Extraverts anyway, so they appear especially warm, though the important decisions will be made by their objective Thinking function, which the world does not see so much of since it is Introverted. So these tough decisions, blunt actions and statements, may come as a surprise to friends or co-workers.

"Shadow Side" 4th Function — Ni — Introverted iNtuition is the ESTP's 4th or least-developed function, the potential source of great insights, and of getting them into much trouble. It shows itself as gloom and doom, over-preparedness for unlikely disasters to come. Unrealistic, it can occasionally be wildly optimistic, but is more likely to mire the ESTP in total pessimism, and encourage undervaluing of the self. They may need help in envisioning positive possibilities for themselves in general and in particular situations.

SP— Flexible realists, they work and play with great style, a smooth perfection and suavity that they develop naturally by doing. The Spanish have a term— *gracia*— doing things with a sort of grace that ESTPs epitomize regardless of the pressure. The higher the stakes the better, for they love risk-taking. They are at times generous to a fault, for they operate so spontaneously that they give in to the latest urge, which may be to make a truly grand and extravagant gesture. There is a theatricality about many ESTPs. They handle themselves so comfortably that it seems they are performing at all times, and in a sense they are. They love to be the center of attention.

ST— Logical and practical, they are good with numbers and matters financial. Not greatly interested in theory unless they see the practical value of its application, they tend to succeed more in life than in school— thanks to our school system, which does not teach them the way they learn best. We drive many out at an early stage, where they often demonstrate how much of importance they have learned, that we do not teach or test children on. Those that pursue advanced education often opt for practical courses and careers rather than theory and ideas.

EP— As action-oriented **Extraverts** and flexible **Perceivers,** ESTPs are especially good at dealing spontaneously with whatever the world may throw at them. They are the height of flexible comfort and move easily in the environment.

TP— Thinking Perceivers can be deceptive, since they base their major decisions on logic, but do this inwardly, quietly. (They *need* quiet, preferably alone time, for optimum decision-making.) But because they Extravert their Feeling function, the world sees them as warm teddy-bear types, and can be surprised or even blind-sided by a decision that ignores Feeling considerations.

ESTP Life Themes— ESTPs have a tendency to follow the irresistible impulse, seeking to experience new and exciting physical sensations. Sports and physical things, equipment and the like, often play a part in their lives. They live in the here and now, and are consummate realists, to the point of being blunt. Their theatrical style lends grace; whatever they do is done with panache. There is often an entrepreneurial bent in an ESTP. They often love practical jokes.

How to Spot ESTPs— Look for a theatrical Extravert, always on the move (sitting too long is a no-no)— a practical, usually hands-on person who can handle almost any external situation with style and flair. They may have command of a vast storehouse of facts on things in which they are interested, usually practical, physical things (e.g., engine specifications in all the latest car models, stats on sports teams, or their business). Charming, friendly and approachable, their logical side may nonetheless sometimes hurt others' feelings unintentionally.

Gender Differences— There is often a macho flavor to a male ESTP, and a tomboy air about a female. Part of this is simply the preference for Thinking over Feeling; but the sensation-seeking SP Temperament multiplies it. In maturity this is modified somewhat, as the ESTP's natural flair provides a generally smooth interface with the world.

ESTP Key Words

action	suave	to the point	fun
charm	variety	flexible	good in crises
doers	concrete	adventuresome	ignore rules
energetic	here-and-now	clever	improvisers
enthusiastic	observant	entrepreneur	impulsive
friendly	conditional	excitement	risk-takers
outgoing	straight-talking	freedom-loving	dramatic

© 1994 William DG Murray PO Box 200 Gladwyne PA 19035-0200 USA

ESTJ—Extraverted Thinker with Introverted Sensing

Overview— ESTJs are classic executive types. They are action-oriented doers who deal logically and realistically with all the facts, data, things and people in the environment, and do so in a well-planned and organized way, on time and under budget. They are constantly organizing the facts and checking their checklists. This executive style often extends into their personal life, with a mix of positive and negative effects.

As Dominant Thinkers their time focus is a logical linear past-to-present-to-future flow. They basically live today, using the experience of the past to plan for the future. ESTJs are about 12% of the U.S. population.

ESTJs are Extraverted, Sensing, Thinking and Judging— Extraverted Thinkers, who when they deal with the inner world prefer to use their practical Sensing to process data.

E— ESTJs focus their considerable energies on the outer world of things, data and people. Hard workers, they like variety and company. (They need someone to delegate tasks to, their natural tendency.) They prefer to work with others.

Si— Sensing is their **Auxiliary** or second-most preferred function. **Introverted**, it takes a bit longer to operate, time the ESTJ may decide not to allow—in which case a decision may be made *too* quickly, with inadequate information.

ESTJs' five senses provide them clear, detailed current input on what the world is about. Thus they feel they can rely on facts (reality as they see it or have experienced it; or by extension, matters about which a reliable authority assures them). So they focus on the here-and-now, and are expert at dealing practically with it. ESTJs prefer physical things and facts to theoretical possibilities and ideas.

Te— Their **Dominant Extraverted Thinking** function makes most ESTJ decisions, using logic to compare things with the basic Rules & Regulations of Life that are programed into their mind. They see things analytically, cooly, objectively, and tend to be more interested in things than people. (Things are more successfully dealt with using the rules of logic, a practice that can lead to great frustration if applied to feisty humans.)

As Extraverts they may think out loud, using their Dominant Thinking judgment process. So what you *hear* may be a first tentative solution to a problem, but expressed as a final logical decision; it *sounds* unarguably cast in bronze, complete with schedule and assignments for *you* to do.

ESTJs may also get in the habit of making decisions for people, enjoy it, and extend the habit into areas where their expertise is limited and their quick decisions not so reliable!

J— As **Judgers**, ESTJs do like to have things decided. They want to be in control, or at least know that some capable person is. It's part of their basic security, which includes punctuality, neatness, order and organization, in their own lives, and their expectations about yours.

Their instrument of control is the Plan. Usually written, at least in part, it includes daily prioritized lists of Things to Do, which are normally completed, in order, and checked off. When for some reason the plan is derailed, everything stops until a new plan, however basic, can be outlined. They are capable of planning, scheduling, and dealing with vast amounts of data and organizing monumental enterprises down to the smallest detail; or plotting their vacation sightseeing on a 3x5 card. All it takes is a plan to be sure that everything gets done optimally.

All this efficiency makes for practical effectiveness and ultimate recognition in the real world; ESTJs often rise to managerial positions, and are usually good providers.

Ne— ESTJs usually **Extravert** their **3rd function, iNtuition**. Since they tend to Extravert often, they may develop it quite well, and may appear to be ENTJs.

"Shadow Side" 4th Function — Fi The fourth and least-preferred or "shadow function" for ESTJs is **Feeling** and it is **Introverted**, so it gets little use. When the ESTJ is constantly Extraverting, it is necessarily shut down, locked in the unconscious. At midlife it may assert itself powerfully, if inopportunely, often by compelling feelings of passionate love for some new, usually totally inappropriate, individual. If the ESTJ does not understand what this really means (it has to do with his own developmental needs) he may think he is really in love, and do real harm to his life, career, and family.

SJ— Pillars of the community, ESTJs usually feel duty-bound to extend their managerial talents to churches and other institutions that need their help. Their lives are run by the rules, and the rules include a responsibility to others as well as themselves. Commitments are real and normally honored loyally and dutifully. Often called the "economic" Temperament, SJs tend to be quite conscious of costs and the value of money.

ST— The ESTJ's combination of pragmatic **Sensing** with logical **Thinking** makes for practical effectiveness in large organizations and careers like accounting, law, engineering, management, which use large amounts of data logically.

EJ— Those who prefer **Extraversion** and **Judging** like to "organize the environment." They focus on the outer world and try to organize it and fit it into their plans and schedules. There is a focus on quick action and decisiveness that works wonders in difficult situations. Using their S and T to get information and call the shots, they make things happen!

TJ— Most top executives in large organizations are TJs— **Thinkers** and **Judgers**— who make quick, logical decisions. ESTJs are probably the most populous in this group, and among attorneys and judges, able to make decisions without looking back or being slowed by second thoughts. TJs are "the four sharp corners of the Type Table" (see page 151); they can be brusque and hurt people's feelings unintentionally. If told of this, they may well decide it is the other person's fault (a tendency that ultimately can provide them with much alone time to think). The prescription, most often sought at midlife, but better if started sooner, is to find ways to let the less-preferred parts of the personality out to play from time to time.

ESTJ Life Themes— ESTJs believe above all in logic, in the power of the Thinking function. Everything is judged with that logic yardstick. A recurrent theme is the later realization that there is more, a Feeling dimension to life, and the beautiful, sometimes painful, process of befriending it— or painfully, disastrously trying to ignore, squelch, or deny it.

Another theme is the growth of the individual career and the building of a family, obeying all the rules and reaping life's rewards for loyal service and dutiful commitment.

How to Spot ESTJs— ESTJs are usually busy, social, civic-minded and active. Evident extraversion makes it easier to spot their other functions, especially the unmistakeable Thinking judgment that they lead with most of the time. Judgments, conclusions, briefly stated, often critical, based on logic; not warm fuzzy "wonderful!" and "fantastic!" preferred by Feelers. They are clean-desk folks. Organization is their middle name. Almost everything in their life is neat and organized, down to their little address book.

Gender Differences— ESTJ men are stereotypical males—they may be "macho" types— so ESTJ females have even more of the

Thinking women's upstream swimming. At best, ESTJ women can be a powerful combination of tough executive, socialized to be as warm and feminine as possible— the iron fist in the velvet glove. At worst, they may be torn between two conflicting poles of softness vs. toughness.

ESTJ men may be so stereotypical that they do not develop their softer side, and though financially successful, they may struggle painfully with family and relationships. At best, they may develop their own Feeling side, especially at midlife, and find themselves more effective on all fronts.

ESTJ Key Words

action	reason	civic	parental
charm	control	commitment	policy
outgoing	decisive	conscientious	possessions
concrete	discipline	conservators	procedures
doers	follow-through	dependable	rituals
facts	orderly	duty	rules & regulations
no-nonsense	organized	earnest	should, ought
practical	persistent	executive	tradition
analytical	punctual	hard-working	black and white
impersonal	schedules	hierarchical	clear roles
logical	structure	institutions	conclusions
principles	businesslike	loyal	take charge

ISFJ—Introverted Senser with Extraverted Feeling

Overview— ISFJs (about 6% of the population) are warm, caring, loyal, service-oriented, organized and neat, realistic, practical, and conservative with money. They tend to put others' welfare first, and may be taken advantage of at times.

As Dominant Sensers, their time focus is right here and now, today's reality. They relate the present to the traditional past; they may need help to plan for the future.

ISFJs are Introverted, Sensing, Feeling and Judging— Introverted Sensers, who when they deal with the outer world prefer to use their values-oriented Feeling function.

I— As **Introverts**, ISFJs prefer to live inwardly. Only those closest to them are aware of the depth, beauty and richness of their inner resources. They are quiet and thoughtful. They usually have a few very close friends of long standing, though many who appreciate them.

Si— **Introverted Sensing** is their **Dominant** (#1) function, the guiding principle in their life; but because it is focused inwardly, few others see it, certainly not in its true power. They are interested in the facts, all the facts. They take in vast amounts of information through their five senses, in exquisite detail, and can recall it easily. They are practical, economic, common-sense, step-by step, reality-based people.

Fe— Warm, **Extraverted Feeling**, the **Auxiliary** function, is what most people see of the ISFJ. Thus some may appear to be Extraverts because of this warmth. They are caring, "What can I do for you?" people. After they consider the facts, their decisions are based on their unique personal value system— what is right or wrong, good or bad, how will it affect the people involved? Their speech is full of Feeling judgments, usually positive ones, but sometimes complaints when they have been taken advantage of, which happens because of their deep caring, strong work ethic, and sense of duty and responsibility. They are perhaps the most susceptible to being codependent.

J— ISFJs are organized, thorough, detailed, super-dependable. Generally decisive with day-to-day matters, they may take a long time making important decisions; they want more facts first. Good with children, they nevertheless tend to be serious, especially until *all* the work is done!

Ti— ISFJs' **3rd function Thinking** is less preferred than Feeling, and is **Introverted**, so we seldom see evidence of its use, especially where women have been socialized strongly toward the Feeling side. Quiet time is needed for ISFJs to access their Thinking, another reason for their desire to take more time with important decisions.

Ne— **iNtuition** is an ISFJ's **"Shadow Side" fourth function.** Not often exercised, it tends to be used extravertedly when it is used. It may show as a quirky sense of humor, even an occasional pun. ISFJs are not big on "the vision thing;" ISFJ President George Bush took much flak for this tendency. This reflects ISFJs' least-developed function, extraverted iNtuition, which looks into future possibilities for them— but does so poorly, seeing few possibilities, mostly bad, and causing a "doom and gloom" tendency which they must work to overcome. It can lead them into depression when they are in its clutches. (In mild cases, getting back into preferred Sensing, e.g., by hands-on activities like gardening, crewel or woodworking, can help.)

SJ— ISFJs are often pillars of the community and their church, helping people and organizations and contributing their time and energy to worthy causes. They are responsible citizens, hard workers, aware of the "shoulds" and "oughts" of life, following the rules and expecting the same of others. They are "economic" folk, aware of the value of the dollar, and smart shoppers.

SF— As SFs, ISFJs are warm, people-oriented, and practical. Their charity is often person-to person— hands-on, local, rather than global appeals. They will quietly help the neighbor next door in time of need, and never tell anyone. They are perhaps the most loyal of all Types, and stand by their friends and their commitments.

IJ— As **Introverted Judgers**, they deal with the outer world fairly quickly and decisively, especially on minor matters. But their true preference is for Sensing, a perceiving function, so they really like more information, and on important matters will take much more time to decide. They probably have warm smiles, but most of the time they are in their Introverted mode, and appear more serious.

FJ— The Feeling function, especially with female ISFJs, usually gets a fair amount of exercise, and they may have well-developed people skills. They speak in value judgments, often enthusiastically.

ISFJ Life Themes— Order and restrained good taste, caring and concern for others, doing their duty responsibly and loyally, quietly working hard to serve those they love and are committed to, are all ISFJ life themes. They need to be needed. They may work too hard, be taken advantage of; but they would rather that than shirk their duty or leave someone in the lurch.

ISFJs can be worry-warts; they collect worries, their own and those of their friends. Their shadow iNtuition sees the downside, as we noted. With their own worries, it can be hard to dissuade them of the gloomy outlook. But with a friend who comes to them with a worry, they may turn on their Extraverted Feeling, and try to help the friend see the bright side! The ISFJ's Feeling and iNtuition combine to find a few good prospects, and they may help the friend feel better, quit worrying. The ISFJ, however, may well keep worrying for the friend.

How to Spot ISFJs— ISFJs are the warm, caring, overburdened workers everyone else tries to get working late so they can go home. They are neat, organized and orderly, quiet and unassuming, caring and helpful, dutiful and loyal to a fault. They are always writing little personal notes to people, prompt thank-you's and hello-I-was-just thinking of-you's. They can be counted on to "do the necessary." Because they want to prepare for the worst, they may have a full refrigerator and food supply cabinet stocked to survive a long winter.

Gender Differences— ISFJ females are perhaps stereotypically feminine— quiet, caring, warm, doing well the tasks of a homemaker.

Male ISFJs may have a harder time figuring out how to be who they are, and may be powerfully trained to be quite the opposite— e.g., President Bush's youthful macho exploits as a fighter pilot.

ISFJ Key Words

quiet	nurturer	dependable
reflective	thoughtful	doom & gloom
"getter-doner"	undemanding	duty
factual knowledge	unselfish	family
literal	values	hard worker
realistic	neat	obedient
simplicity	orderly	respect authority
steady	timely	responsible
caring	commitment	service
generous	conform to the rules	stability
giving	conscientious	super-dependable
harmonious	consistent	thorough
kind & gentle	conventional roles	work first, play later
making others happy		

ISFP—Introverted Feeler with Extraverted Sensing

Overview— ISFPs are friendly, carefree, unassuming realists, flexible, often unconventional, but with considerable grace and style. Their strong passions, values and sensitivities are internal— not always evidenced except with close friends.

As Dominant Introverted Feelers their time focus is the past, where they have experienced good feelings before; they always try to recreate these positive experiences. As Sensers, they are very here and now, focused on the present, especially when they are Extraverting. ISFPs are about 6% of the U.S. population.

ISFPs are Introverted, Sensing, Feeling and Perceiving— Introverted Feelers, who when they deal with the outer world prefer to use their practical Sensing function.

I— Introverts, ISFPs are quiet, modest and self-effacing, but with great inner depth which they rarely share and may have difficulty expressing. There is more complexity than meets the eye, especially since the world sees the part (Sensing) that strives for simplicity, economy of action, line or form.

Se— Their **Auxiliary** function, **Sensing** is **Extraverted**; their five senses provide them a constant input of experience— concrete facts and details— which they assimilate and use as a basis for decisions. They tend to speak in literal practical terms; even their occasional metaphor is likely to be concrete —e.g., dead as a doornail. ISFPs are hands-on, experiential, often tactile people, and they are often skilled in a variety of crafts requiring manual dexterity as well as the performing arts.

Fi— Feeling is the real captain of their ship, the **Dominant** part that calls the shots in their life; but it is **Introverted**; its presence is only occasionally evident to the world outside. ISFPs are sensitive, sentimental, passionate people, but only those very close to them are privy to this part. They may in fact not show much affect, while inside much is going on. ISFPs seek inner harmony above all else, and it is not easy to find, or even articulate. They have an ideal that finds expression most often either in a very close relationship, or in support of a powerfully held ideal, particularly one being attacked. They may then change from the gentlest of all the Types, to an obstinately powerful person to be reckoned with.

Generally they do not seek to stand out or take charge, unless there is chaos and they can see clearly what must be done. Then they "just do it" as the Nike commercial said.

ISFPs hold their inner ideals and values with a certainty and conviction that is virtually unshakeable. They experience criticism of these as deeply personal and wounding. They may respond with total withdrawal or counterattack, either of which may come as a surprise to the critic, who may have been simply trying to be helpful.

P— As **Perceiving** Types, ISFPs are flexible, unhurried, tolerant individuals, often free spirits. They are open minded (unless you step on their values!) and willing to entertain a variety of viewpoints. (They will probably prefer whatever works.) They can adapt well when things are in flux; their sense of reality keeps them well grounded and their Perception keeps them open and non-directive. So they make good counselors, especially crisis and hotline counselors.

Ni— **Introverted iNtuition** is an ISFP's **3rd function**, key input that outlines options for consideration and decision-making by the Dominant Feeling. From age 18 to midlife it grows in impact, but is rarely seen by others.

"Shadow Side" 4th Function — Te — Extraverted Thinking is the "shadow side" of the ISFP. When in its throes they can be cold and critical. Logic and the rational, impersonal approach do not come easily to them, though they may develop them in time because life demands it. But they will always be subject to being blindsided by negative "spurious conclusions" (which they are stubbornly convinced are valid) about themselves, their own capability and self-worth. ISFPs are especially subject to feelings of low self-esteem, because they are so vulnerable to criticism to begin with, and because in school they are taught in a learning style foreign to them. Like all SPs, they may be accused of Attention Deficit Disorder, hyperactivity, or other learning disabilities due to their natural style and the ignorance of those in charge.

SP— ISFPs are able to deal with chaos and crisis because they are so grounded in what is happening right now. They do the necessary, the most important thing, then the next. They don't stop to plan, which might waste precious seconds (or months, as the case may be). They may have the soul of an adventurer, and the performing skill of a virtuoso. They are willing to practice endlessly to perfect a move or a skill, be it tennis, violin, painting or woodcarving. Their persistence is legendary— so long as they are interested in what they're doing. Once the (sometimes impulsive) motivation passes, they may move on. ISFPs can be world-class performers: mimes, musicians, actors and acrobats, dancers, athletes— their gross motor muscles are often exceptionally well trained and give them a grace of movement and style that makes hard things look effortless.

As SPs, they are activity-oriented; sitting still to read or talk is not their favorite thing, especially young ISFPs. (Later they may become avid readers, when they can pick their own topics.) They may have trouble in schools that are not oriented to teach the way they learn: in a warm, flexible, hands-on experiential way, stressing the practical applications of a theory, not what a beautiful theory it is. Classroom regimentation drives them out, often with their good friends, to find some action, if school doesn't provide any. Their sense of esprit de corps and loyalty— to a group, to family— can be strong.

SF— ISFPs are interested in other people, and they are generally warm, caring and helpful. They are more interested in local charity, helping their neighbors, than in global causes that inspire iNtuitives.

IP— Introverted Perceivers are "closet Judgers." That is, their strongest, most preferred function is a Judging function— for ISFPs, Feeling judgment. So while they are generally very flexible, easy to deal with, even take advantage of, this casualness stops abruptly at the edge of their values and ideals; step on a value, and they are suddenly decisive, immovable, obstinate.

FP— Gentlest of the sixteen Types, ISFPs are symbolized by St. Francis of Assisi, a loving, gentle man who communed with nature and communicated with birds and small animals. Many veterinarians and their staff are ISFP. They can be very vulnerable to criticism or hurt by those close to them, so may take special care not to open up until they are sure it is safe.

ISFP Life Themes— ISFPs spend much introverted time working on their own personal values, determining what really matters. They relate strongly to whatever or whomever fits this description, and their key relationship(s) are especially vital to them, though they are not so outwardly expressive of this as an Extravert would be. But should there be any problem or threat to such a one, they will be there ready to defend him or her (or it, if it be a value) most determinedly.

How to Spot ISFPs— Introverts, being Introverts, are generally harder to spot than Extraverts. Some ISFPs may even be deceptively active and congenial, in the right company, and may appear Extraverted. They will be gentle, caring people, lovers of nature and animals; as SPs, activity-oriented, carefree, fun, often hands-on in style. Fun is important to them, at work or play. Self-effacing, and usually unassertive, they do not push themselves to the front. They tend to speak in perceptions, not judgments, usually with simple, straightforward facts, in literal and descriptive statements.

Gender Differences— Male ISFPs are at a disadvantage as gentle FP Types, and this may lead them to emphasize the Introverted Sensing (IS)—strong, silent, macho, hands-on practical side of their nature. Their Dominant Feeling, Introverted though it be, is still in charge, but the macho side may overrun it on occasion, especially with younger ISFPs. ISFP women often get less acceptance of their free spirit SP nature, and may find more outlets for their gentle side, which is truly predominant. But as this is Introverted, they may be quieter overall than the males when they take this direction.

ISFP Key Words

complexity	tactile	supportive	dexterity
concentration	certainty	tactful	effortless
contemplation	conviction	values	esprit de corps
inner depth	duty	adaptable	fun
modest	empathy	free spirit	hands-on
quiet	ideals	nondirective	independent
reserved	inner harmony	open	lighthearted
unassuming	loyal	relaxed	mime
activities	passion	tolerant	performer
concrete	peace	unhurried	persistence
details	personal	active	unconventional
experiential	praise	adventure	wanderlust
here-and-now	sensitive	carefree	gentle
pragmatic	sentiment	crafts	vulnerable

ESFP—Extraverted Sensers with Introverted Feeling

Overview— ESFPs are sociable, friendly "people people," action folks who are good in a crisis, talented performers of all sorts who can get things done despite adverse circumstances.

As Dominant Sensers their time focus is the here-and-now present; more than any other Type, they live each moment.

ESFPs are Extraverted, Sensing, Feeling and Perceiving— Extraverted Sensers, who when they deal with their inner world prefer to use their Feeling function. ESFPs are 12% of theU.S. population.

E— Extraverted, outgoing and friendly, helpful "good buddy" to a wide circle of friends, the ESFP is a sociable party person even when working prodigiously. (Work and play should both be fun, and ESFPs make them fun. Their play may not be relaxing but physically taxing; but it will not feel like work.) ESFPs live in the outer world and what's going on there tends to determine their life as they react to it. They are at ease in the environment, and are comfortable as performers of all sorts: musical, theatrical, athletic. They carry things off with remarkable personal grace, style and flair.

Se— Sensing, aimed **Extravertedly** at the outer world, is an ESFP's **Dominant** and strongest function, the one that runs their life and provides them with their greatest satisfaction. Their well-developed five senses are constantly monitoring the environment, providing input of factual data: *what's happening*. This is what's real, and ESFPs are supreme realists, pragmatists. Skip the theory; these are the facts— what will really work? So let's *do* it! Their Extraversion lends action orientation, and the doing is almost one with the perception of the situation. In a crisis, they leap in and instinctively do what needs to be done to prevent disaster, while other Types are analyzing and weighing possible consequences of each option. Walter Lowen notes that ESFPs tend to have excellent gross motor muscle skills, which gives them athletic potential as well as the physical ability for crisis interventions that need it.

They are very observant, and store a great many facts, usually relating to people or to objects (which their Feeling may tend to personalize— sometimes literally, as pilots give names to their planes or truckers to their trucks).

Sensing makes them practical, commonsense folks. They don't spend much time on theory or planning if they can avoid it.

Fi— Their **Auxiliary** function, **Feeling** judgment makes ESFPs' decisions, but it is **Introverted**, so they tend not to broadcast their judgments on things. (That might not be harmonious, anyway, and Feelers need harmony in everything they do.) ESFPs are warm teddy bears and try to avoid criticism or disagreement; disharmony makes them anxious. In fact, if there is a disagreement, they are likely to change the subject, discover a need to do something that short-circuits the discussion, feign agreement passive-aggressively, depart, or otherwise ignore the controversy. This makes them successful politicians, who get elected by avoiding strong stands and being foursquare in favor of all positions as long as possible, and working out harmonious compromise when it gets down to the wire. ESFPs can be skilled negotiators.

P— As **Perceivers**, ESFPs are flexible and spontaneous— at times too impulsive. They are laid-back and casual, enjoy a good time at work or play, and may be hard to tie down for decisions, which would reduce their options.

Te— **Thinking**, their **3rd function**, is usually **Extraverted** with ESFPs, so they may well give you logical reasons in support of a decision that was already made (for Feeling reasons) by their Introverted Feeling process. The cool logic may or may not prevail, but these are not their true reasons. If the logic is faulty (it is their third-best function), they may be marked down by some, who do not know the true and valid basis for the ESFP's judgment.

"Shadow Side" 4th Function — Ni—The ESFP's least developed side is i**Ntuition**, and it is **Introverted**. They are not much interested in theory unless they see a practical use for it. When they try to examine possibilities, they tend to see few, usually unrealistically bad or good. This can increase their anxiety level or depress them, so they may try to shift out of iNtuition and get back to familiar Sensing, their strongest suit (digging in the yard, working with tools or the like should do it).

SP— **Sensing Perceivers** are practical and spontaneous. They have a basic need to feel an impulse, and quickly act on it, before it goes away. ESFPs can be impulsively generous.

They are not usually interested in school, in part because our schools do not teach the way they learn, and the regimented style of most schools drives them up the wall— or out the door. They generally do much better in life than in school— often better than the teacher who failed them, or the counselor who thought their normal SP behavior was "hyperactive" and suggested tranquilizers; but many miss the opportunity that an education would have given them. This is a major problem (and opportunity) in education today:

wasting so many young minds with so much unrecognized talent.

SF— As **Sensing Feelers**, ESFPs are warm, caring and focused on doing specific practical things to be helpful to other individuals, usually friends, neighbors or local causes; they are less interested in faraway problems, however dire, that they cannot see or feel a connection with. ESFPs do countless little things for people, whenever they see the need, and do not keep score.

EP— As **Extraverted Perceivers**, ESFPs focus on the outer world, and want as much information as possible about it. Specifically, ESFPs want factual information, usually about people, or the things in which they are interested.

FP— As **Feeling Perceivers**, ESFPs are gentle types. They decide with their soft, subjective Feeling judgment, but do it slowly and internally, and do not usually force their conclusions on others.

ESFP Life Themes— ESFPs are warm, often physical, and impulse-driven. Delayed gratification is not their thing. Life is a party, or should be, as much of the time as possible. ESFPs can work tirelessly to perfect a skill or a sport to world class levels that look deceptively effortless, provided they feel motivated to do it. Solid tangible facts are the only reality for them, and they are super-realists, as stated earlier. Because most schools do not teach the way they learn, they often leave formal education with a low opinion of their own capacities, and expecting little of themselves, may not achieve what they might have had they gained a better understanding of their own talents.

How to Spot ESFPs— Sociable, party people, often discussing detailed facts about people or their favorite kinds of things, getting a lot of gusto out of life (as in beer commercials, which seem to love stereotypical ESFPs). They are casual, laid-back, able to deal with chaos effectively while others are trying to develop a plan to approach it. They live right now, smell today's daisies. Theories and futures are not for them— except possibly commodity futures, where the frantic nature of the trading pit is just their cup of tea.

Gender Differences— As Feelers and Perceivers, the ESFP's gentleness and caring make them excellent in serving others, in dealing with children (where they are truly brilliant). Our society seems to think this is OK for women (albeit not high-pay OK) but not very masculine for male ESFPs. Judgers may see ESFPs' flexibility as "wishy-washy," downgrade them as flaky (men or women), and miss an advantage that could help them.

Some male ESFPs choose macho occupations like

firefighters, where there is group comraderie and physical activity in a crisis atmosphere, but time to have a good social time, also.

ESFP Key Words

action	appreciate	compromise
activity	considerate	crisis
doing	harmony	diplomat
empirical	helpful	easygoing
energy	interpersonal	enjoyment
enthusiasm	positive	esprit de corps
excitement	sensitive	fashionable
experience	supportive	generous
make things happen	sympathy	good buddies
optimism	voluble	hustle
zest	warm	hyperactive
5 senses	accepting	immediate
common sense	easy-going	impulsive
concrete	flexible	jolly
down-to-earth	fun	just do it!
facts	laid-back	mediator
here and now	least resistance	overextended
matter-of-fact	play	party
observant	playful	risk
practical	procrastination	service
realistic	athletics	smooth
specific	charming	sophistication
step-by-step	clever	spontaneous
tangible	comfort	wheeler-dealer
aesthetics		

ESFJ—Extraverted Feeler with Introverted Sensing

Overview— ESFJs are warm, caring, sociable people who focus primarily on human relationships and the mutual expression of positive feelings. They are the "hostess (or host) with the mostest," the Social Director of the Love Boat who arranges events, finds out detailed information about the passengers, and introduces those with things in common. As Dominant Feelers their time focus is in the past (whose good feelings they try to recreate in the present); as here-and-now Sensers they are able to "smell the daisies."

ESFJs are Extraverted, Sensing, Feeling and Judging— Extraverted Feelers, who when they deal with the inner world prefer to use their practical Sensing function.

E— ESFJs are outgoing, friendly **Extravert** types at home in the environment of people and things. Especially people. Sociable masters of relationships, their lives are filled with meetings, conversations and activities with their long list of friends. They are excellent as teachers, salespersons, and in caring professions such as nursing or medicine. ESFJs are about 12% of the U.S. population.

Si— **Introverted Sensing** is the ESFJ's second-strongest or **Auxiliary** function, and it runs their inner life. It gives them a constant flow of real-time, concrete, factual information on which to base their decisions—which thus tend to be practical, commonsense, and realistic, provided the ESFJ introverts enough to have developed this Auxiliary. (Some ESFJs are so social and so fill their lives with external activity that their Sensing is not well developed, and they may base decisions on faulty data.) Also, ESFJs may *deny* facts their Dominant Feeling function finds disagreeable. This allows them to maintain surface harmony, but may ultimately lead to disastrous decisions, since facts tend not to go away when ignored.

Fe— **Extraverted Feeling** is the heart of the ESFJ, the **Dominant** function the world sees from them most of the time. It runs the show. Its primary goal is warm feelings from relationships with others; it tries to make others feel good, lovingly serving others' needs, on the assumption that they will return the favor. Of course, no good deed is left unpunished; the others may find it impossible to live up to the expectations the ESFJ has laid upon them, if only because they are too busy enjoying being waited upon to think of reciprocating. In fact this much love may foster dependency in friends, mate and children. The ESFJ idealizes— the other person, or even the organization they serve and nurture— and ignores or denies any negative information that others might observe about the object of their interest. The ESFJ may eventually feel resentful, while still serving selflessly, and never tending to his or her own needs. Extraverted Feelers are among the most at risk of codependency, since they are so intent upon harmony, on expressing love and receiving it in return.

J— ESFJs are Extraverted **Judgers**, who decide things very quickly —not so much because they enjoy the process, but because they feel more secure once things are decided. They may decide too quickly, and be reluctant to reopen a matter once decided. ESFJs usually are not power-seekers, but they may jump in and start deciding everything if they feel no one else will do it on the ESFJ's timetable. They may then seem bossy, for they fear consequences if they do not move in.

They do have timetables, and schedules, usually busy ones. They may tend to fill their time with appointments and opportunities to Extravert, rather than spend much time Introverting, which though necessary can make them uncomfortable (see "Shadow Side" below).

Ne— ESFJs tend to **Extravert** their **3rd function iNtuition**, so may appear to be ENFJs to a casual observer, particularly if they get little Introversion time to develop their preferred Sensing. But they tend to be practical rather than abstract, and enjoy the past and present more than live in the future.

"Shadow Side" 4th Function — Ti — Introverted Thinking is the ESFJ's least preferred and least developed function. At its best it is a useful help in problem solving and important decisions, understanding of cause and effect and adding a note of objectivity in judgment. This requires considerable effort, Thinking, and more Introverted time than many ESFJs like.

It can also get ESFJs into trouble. First, by the absence of understanding, e.g., of what logically will happen if ESFJs take some action that they desperately *want* to take, or by providing rationalizations only for actions their Feeling has already decided on. Second, by its tendency to provide *spurious conclusions*, based on faulty logic, usually harsh negative judgments about themselves, friends or family. They are convinced these conclusions are absolutely true. In the throes of shadow Thinking, their warm Feeling is locked up and they can be astonishingly cold, even verbally cruel to loved ones.

SJ— ESFJs are traditionalists, conserving the best of the past. They may like rituals and established ways of doing things. They can handle a considerable amount of routine sucessfully, provided there is harmony. They can be counted on to do what they promised. Very loyal and hard-working, they are super dependable and excellent at follow-through.

Economic types, they are usually aware of the value of money and are conservative financial managers, able to save for the future and delay gratification— if their Sensing is functioning well to deliver the facts, and their Feeling is not denying those facts in order to do what it wants to do.

SF— ESFJs combine practical **Sensing** with a **Feeling** people focus, so they are very effective with practical people matters, individual human care and attention.

EJ— As **Extraverted Judgers**, ESFJs are always "organizing the environment." They focus on people and things, not theories and ideas, and they want to get everything settled, organized, so all will go smoothly. They usually have an excellent sense of what has gone on at a meeting, and are well equipped to summarize it impressively.

As Extraverts, they think out loud, and what they express mostly is a string of Feeling judgments. As a thought process, this may be a bit fuzzy and rambling, unlike an Introvert who thinks through everything clearly before speaking. It will of course all *sound* like final decisions, even if still tentative, which can discourage Feelers' gentle disagreements and make a Thinker's more critical, to the ESFJ's dismay.

FJ— Because they Extravert their **Feeling judgment**, they "wear their heart on their sleeves." They are very open and expressive, and come across as warm and caring people, which they truly are. Feeling that is Extraverted relates to everything in the external world, asking, "How do I relate to that?" and doing its best to establish a connection, a warm relationship with the other. As a result, their focus and affections may be widely spread, expended over a broad circle of friends and casual acquaintances, so that family and those closest to the ESFJ may at times feel like the last in line.

ESFJ Life Themes— Relationships are perhaps the primary theme for ESFJs. They have, as van der Hoop put it, "a vital need to find corresponding feelings in others," to connect in feeling relationships, often with someone whom they idealize, as they idealize(d) their parents. Projections are often their deepest reality.

Harmony is a Feeler's theme, especially for ESFJs. They need, seek, and effectively create harmony wherever they go. Without it they may be significantly disabled.

Appropriateness is another ESFJ theme: always to be appropriate— appropriately dressed, coifed, housed, driving appropriate cars, in an appropriate occupation— and so on.

How to Spot ESFJs— ESFJs are warm, sociable, friendly, appropriately attired (often a bit on the formal side). At a board meeting with ten women, only the two ESFJs wore makeup. They also wore skirts and hose, and felt comfortable.

ESFJs have many friends with whom they are in frequent phone or direct contact. Much time is spent in conversation— working on projects, or relationships, or both.

Gender Differences— ESFJ characteristics are stereotypically female. "Warm caring mother " is fine for female ESFJs, who have many role models and can feel OK being who they are. Male ESFJs have it harder. They are likely to be more assertive than the females, but less so than an ESTJ. As males they may have the advantage of developing their Thinking earlier than female ESFJs (though it is still #4 in strength), and their powerful Feeling side is far ahead of Thinking males'.

ESFJ Key Words

outgoing	helpful	warmth	loyal
concrete	idealize	decisive	melancholy
details	nostalgic	expectations	parental
here and now	nurturing	follow-through	respectful
matter-of-fact	people	orderly	responsible
practical	personalize	persistence	rituals
simplicity	praise	punctual	rules
appreciation	relationships	schedule	service
compassion	sensitive	structure	tradition
contacts	strokes	conform	perfect host/hostess
cooperation	sympathetic	conscientious	sociability
demonstrative	tactful	dependable	appropriate
gracious	values	family	modest
harmony	want to please	hierarchical	possessions

INFJ— Introverted iNtuitive with Extraverted Feeling

Overview— INFJs are quiet, creative, caring, and tend to be organized and decisive. They are motivated by their "vision," i.e., the meanings they see and the connections they make in their inner world. This is much like the Extraverted iNtuitive, only the INFJ's iNtuition is usually not visible to others. It is as if they are constructing their own world, comprehending the true essence of things, but must do so with limited access to the outer world in which Extraverts seem so comfortable. They work at, and may get very good at expressing this inner knowledge in ways that others can comprehend. For INFJs this is utter Truth, objective fact. They may tend to limit their personal connections to those who can understand or to some degree share their inner vision. Introverted iNtuition, plus very personal Feeling values, make each INFJ's vision unique. There may be a wider range of personality among INFJs than with any other type. Only about 1% of the population are INFJs.

As Dominant iNtuitives, their time focus is the future. They see with remarkable vision what that future will be, or what they would like it to be, and they plan and work with incredible quiet diligence to make it happen. The future is where they prefer to live.

INFJs are Introverted, iNtuitive, Feeling and Judging— Introverted iNtuitives, who when they deal with the outer world prefer to use their Feeling judgment.

I— INFJs are **Introverts**. They focus internally, and usually keep the best part of themselves inside. They tend to be quiet, soft-spoken, like quiet time to think, and *need* quiet to charge their batteries. If you speak to a silent INFJ, you are probably interrupting.

Ni— INFJs' **Dominant** function, **iNtuition**, is *Introverted*. Most people aren't even vaguely aware of what incredible complexity and Byzantine complication goes on in an INFJ's silence, until some jewel of thought, perfectly polished, is quietly laid upon the table. It is easy to underestimate an INFJ at first. This powerful iNtuition keeps getting better, as more information is added to the inner file system. However, iNtuition is only as good as the data it has to work with. INFJs' may be disadvantaged by a tendency to tune out the outer world, and be slow to develop a comfort in working with real-world people and problems. On the other hand, Introverted iNtuitives usually spend considerable time adding to their storehouse of knowledge through reading and research, giving them a growing advantage over students who stop learning upon (or before) graduation. INFJs are always making connections in their minds, perceiving meaning about the very essence of things that others do not. They read between the lines well. (Though when such a reading is incorrect, they may find it difficult to admit, even to themselves). This is often the source of what can be seen as stubbornness, for their iNtuition is felt inside as pure fact, Truth Absolute. Religious prophets and leaders of Causes are often INFJ, with conviction and courage to pit their vision against king or congress.

Fe— INFJs' **Auxiliary** or secondary function, *Extraverted* Feeling, is used to deal with the outer world. They may tend to speak in judgments of good or bad, like or dislike. They base these judgments on their highly personal value system, which may not agree with those of The System— whatever it may be— where they live or work. When Extraverting that Feeling, INFJs tend to wear out fast, using up their Extraverting fuel quickly. They then need quiet time to "recharge."

J— Though their Dominant (N) is a Perceiving function, they deal with the world using their Extraverted Feeling **Judgment**. This means they like things to be orderly, organized, done "right." They can be the greatest of perfectionists (anything worth doing, is worth doing perfectly). The irony here is, their 4th-function Sensing may be undeveloped, so they may not *observe* things in the environment that they would consider imperfections if they noticed.

Ti— 3rd **function Thinking** judgment is usually **Introverted** for INFJs, and when they need to use this they do well to find some quiet time. Thinking has the advantage of being used in the Introverted attitude in which INFJs tend to spend most of their time, so it can get considerable use. Especially if well trained, their Thinking can be very powerful. Despite being Feelers, INFJs may do well in math or science if so inclined.

"Shadow Side" 4th Function Se— Extraverted Sensing is INFJs' 4th or "shadow function." Least developed, it can be a source of trouble and embarrassment, as when they fail to be sufficiently observant of external reality or facts and so may make an unworkable decision. Their iNtuition provides such variety and complexity inside, that the voice of practical simplicity may get shouted down. An elegantly complicated and thorough plan may have too many opportunities for error or miscalculation. At midlife they may develop their playful SP side, letting their shadow Sensing "out to play." They should beware of a tendency for that Sensing to try to take charge and get them into trouble, especially as expressed in what Isabel Myers called "base sensuality," a powerful calling toward an extra-marital affair. This impulse can be a positive source of energy and personal growth, if recognized and kept within limits. Sensing can also be the key to their deepest spiritual insights, as when close scrutiny and study of a single twig leads to a deep vision of the meaning of life on earth.

NF— As NF "romantics" INFJs are interested in possibilities (N) for people (F); they are likely to be idealists, and may need strong reminding where reality factors are concerned. (And they may nonetheless ignore the advice, and proceed with their own plan for achieving their inner vision.)

NJ— As NJs, INFJs are creative and decisive, though they tend to keep the creativity inside, only revealing their plans or ideas when perfected, and after they have set the stage for them with the people involved. They are given to quiet excellence and often quite refined, restrained taste (never flashy). Their environment is kept in apple-pie order, and don't upset their tablescape or organization; it's part of the way they keep their external environment under control so they can spend more time in their heads.

IJ— INFJs are quiet, thoughtful, planful, and generally decisive. Their verbal communication is likely to be economical, reserved, and brief. Depending on their training, they may show an IJ aloofness and seem hard to get to know, especially if they have not had to develop their auxiliary Extraverted Feeling much.

FJ— However, they do Extravert Feeling judgment, and when this is well developed INFJs may appear to be ENFJs. Usually caring people, INFJs can be quite warm in expressing this, especially to those close to them (women are more likely than men to have developed this warmth). They are warm-hearted, and often extremely thoughtful in terms of finding something special & uniquely meaningful for a friend. However, INFJs are more likely to express warmth verbally than physically; they are rarely "huggy" types, and one should be sensitive not to overstep their boundaries, which are important as part of their defense system.

INFJ Life Themes— INFJs are all unique— even more so than most other types. But they share powerful Introverted iNtuition that gives them a vision, each his or her own. They must follow this vision, and will often do so in the face of all obstacles, advice, or parental effort. Though they may be late starters in life, they are often remarkable achievers.

How to Spot INFJs— Across a room, the INFJ is usually observable as an Introvert, and to a longtime Typespotter™, as an I—J. Besides a calm, quiet demeanor (I) there is usually something that says "J" about them— a feeling of being organized, carefully put together; if casual, carefully casual. All has been planned.

Feeling judgment can be noted in INFJs' speech: often positive (or negative) evaluations, good/bad, like/don't like. INFJs tend to be warm and nurturing, though with many it is in a calm, reserved way.

INFJs may often (though not always) be physically slender, perhaps for a genetic reason related to their type, perhaps because many are disinterested in sports; or they may not stay turned on long to the subtle Sensing benefits of food (they may forget to eat), or may have an enviable metabolism that burns calories rapidly.

Gender Differences— As always, the male tends to be more of the Thinker and the female tends to have Feeling developed more, due to societal expectations (though there are obvious exceptions to this). Women may be quite warm and enthusiastic, especially with friends (though there is always an awareness of boundaries). Male INFJs may evidence their Feeling side more in writing, and in avoidance of disharmony.

INFJ Key Words

aloof	creative	caring	orderly
boundaries	dreamer	easily hurt	organized
depth	freedom	empathy	planful
distance	imagination	gentle	idealistic
hard to know	insight	harmony	inspired
introspective	inspiration	like to be liked	language skills
one-on-one	meaning, significance	loyal	poetic
private	perceptive	personal	romantic
quiet	premonitions	sensitive	perfectionist
rich inner life	prophetic	tactful	tenacious
soft-spoken	psychic	thoughtful	unique
solitude	stimulating	values	
"E.S.P."	vision	warmth	
complex	whimsical	decisive	

Note: For more in-depth treatment of the INFJ, see,"*When ENFP & INFJ Interact,*" by William D. G. Murray & Rosalie R. Murray

INFP— Introverted Feeler with Extraverted iNtuition

Overview— INFPs are value-driven, quiet, idealistic, frequently very spiritual people who can be a powerful moral force in an often unspoken way. They have a sort of invisible "filter" that screens everything and everyone to see if they fit the INFP's central value system. Those that do not pass may never know why they are rejected and can seemingly do no right. The INFP's Feeling-values are internal, and may or may not have been checked out with the "real" (external) world. INFPs may be capable of maintaining values that fly in the face of reality; it is reality that is wrong and must change in such cases. They may accept only those facts that fit their mental picture.

Their values and ideals are central to INFPs and usually define their life scripts. All their actions— careers, relationships and day-to-day behaviors— must be congruent with these values. Their Feeling judgment is Dominant, but Introverted, so only those closest to them get to hear about that side. Others see only the results— the seemingly cast-in-bronze Feeling-based decisions ultimately arrived at after quiet contemplation, that usually will not yield to facts or logical disagreement. Their values represent for them a higher truth, the way things *ought* to be, even if they are not so right now.

As Dominant Feelers, their time focus is the past; as iNtuitives, their Extraverted focus is the future. They often try to recreate the best of the past in the future, so you see them working for social causes.

INFPs are Introverted, iNtuitive, Feeling and Perceiving.

I— INFPs are **Introverts**. They focus on their inner life, and keep their best inside. They tend to be quiet, and need alone time to "charge their batteries" or make important decisions. They may tend to be quite private, and though they may *feel* great warmth and love, they may not always express it, though their mates might wish it. (They may prefer to express it in writing, even poetry, not in spoken words.) INFPs can be a calming presence, easy to be around.

Ne— **Extraverted iNtuition**, the INFP's **Auxiliary** or second-best function, is what they show to the world. They speak in ideas, possibilities, connections, similes and metaphors, stories, questions more than answers. Their iNtuition helps the poet or composer in them to find expression.

Fi— **Introverted Feeling** judgment is the real boss— the **Domi-**

nant function for INFPs. But we do not see it much firsthand, and may be surprised when, after much silent pondering, the INFP unexpectedly states an unshakeable decision. It may not even sound like a decision at first, and it may be reported out by the iNtuition (which makes it sound like another possibility) or the Extraverted Thinking, the least-preferred function, which tries, often badly, to rationalize it with logic. But if that logic is refuted, the decision stands anyway, because it was really not based on logic.

INFPs are gentle and caring, "sensitive plants," whose Dominant Feeling is at once tremendously powerful, but Introverted and restrained. They may feel too vulnerable to express it safely, or it may be simply that it is too diffuse to be expressed with the clarity their perfectionism demands. Later, it may be expressed, as "emotion recollected in tranquillity," (INFP Wordsworth) after it has all been fitted harmoniously into their inner scheme of things.

P— Perceiving is the preferred lifestyle for INFPs: flexible, laid-back, casual, interruptible, more interested in the process than the product. They tend to delay decisions and seek more alternatives. At a restaurant they may be last to order.

But the INFP is a "closet Judger." INFPs really are Dominant Feelers, and Feeling is a deciding function. We just don't *see* that so much. It is Introverted, so it takes a while. But when INFPs do make a decision, especially an important one, it may be very hard to change their stand.

Si— INFPs' **third-preferred** function, **Sensing**, is **Introverted** and not so often expressed verbally. But INFPs may enjoy woodworking and other crafts that make use of this Introverted Sensing in a hands-on way. They can be very fine craftspersons, working slowly but very finely.

"Shadow Side" 4th Function Te— Least-preferred is the INFP's fourth Function **Thinking,** which is **Extraverted** but seldom expressed. It can get the INFP into trouble by providing "spurious conclusions," usually negative, about the competence and value of the INFP as a human being. Often these will seem logical but aren't, being based on faulty logic. It may tie in with the Extraverted iNtuition, giving an overbroad generalization of a small negative judgment.

NF— INFPs are romantic NFs by Temperament. Love songs, poetry and flowers. Often quintessential environmentalists, they are active on behalf of causes to save the planet.

NP— As iNtuitive Perceivers, INFPs Extravert their iNtuition.

They are easily interruptible, and change the subject constantly, especially if there is disharmony to steer away from. They see so many possibilities that they start far more projects than they can finish, at least this lifetime. Paradoxically, if they really enjoy something, it may be especially difficult to complete it; their perfectionism doesn't help, but it is not the sole explanation. They don't want it all to end.

IP— As Introverted Perceivers, INFPs appear flexible, using Perceiving to deal with the world ordinarily. But as noted, their real Commander is Feeling Judgment, and this can be firm to the point of obstinacy when a key value is attacked. It then becomes clear that they are what Jung called "rational" types, dominant deciders, though the process is Introverted and takes longer.

FP— INFPs are gentle Feeling Perceivers, peacemakers, seeking understanding and offering care, helpfulness and their best energies and resources to make the world a better place. Idealists, they are happiest in a career where they are working to this end, even if the pay is low. That's not what's important to them.

INFP Life Themes— Still water runs deep. INFPs have an active inner life that involves their closest relationships and their most passionately supported causes. They can be real leaders in a great cause, though in daily activities they may well hold back from such roles. Most INFPs undervalue themselves because of the unrealistically high standards they set— for life, for love, relationships, and especially for themselves. The world never can live up to their standards for it, but they can forgive it, lick the wounds they've received, and eventually try again. (Or perhaps retire to Walden-like seclusion; Thoreau was an INFP). But their own failings, real or imagined, may bring guilt feelings for which they want to punish themselves or offer themselves as a sacrifice to their cause (or to another person). INFPs make wonderful martyrs— a la INFP Joan of Arc.

How to Spot INFPs— There is frequently something quietly spiritual in the influence of an INFP. They are usually quiet, but may be passionately outspoken on subjects dear to their heart— especially their "causes," which occupy much of their focus. As NPs, they speak in iNtuitive perceptions or possibilities, in often complex simile and metaphor, not simple facts. They may jump from one subject to another without warning or transition. They are basically very gentle and usually concerned for the welfare of other people. They have a perfectionist streak like INFJs, but INFPs may delay completing a job until it is perfect— and it never is. Closure is a problem, including finding a way out of a conversation. They may linger long at the door. Creative and romantic, they are often communicators— writers, poets or composers in one way or another,

Gender Differences— As Dominant Feelers, INFP women are in line with societal expectations for warmth and softness. INFP men are also gentle types, but society expects them to be tough, logical, and "masculine" — i.e., Thinkers. In this regard, they will be swimming upstream all their lives, but may be getting stronger as they go.

INFP Key Words

commitment	calm	considerate	sensitive
complexity	private	conviction	service
control	quiet	devotion	symbolic
cooperation	reserved	empathy	tenderness
determination	reticent	gracious	thoughtful
ethereal	tranquillity	harmony	values
expectations	unobtrusive	honor	vulnerable
integrity	creativity	ideals	acceptance
martyr	daydreaming	impressionistic	adaptable
mask	individual	love	conflict avoidance
moral authority	insights	loyalty	easygoing
obstinacy	visionary	nature	open
perfectionist	better world	peace	passive
persistence	caring	people	pliant
truth-seeker	cause	personalizing	poetry
understanding	certainty	pleasing	self-identity
unpredictable	congenial	relationships	gentle

191

ENFP— Extraverted iNtuition with Introverted Feeling

Overview—An ENFP is an idea machine. A warm, enthusiastic, optimistic, creative problem-solving "teddy bear." A master of possibilities, especially people possibilities. Only 5% of the population are ENFPs. You can often spot one a mile away— but every one is unique. ENFPs don't live here any more; they live in the *future*. They can put up with lots of tough stuff now— because of how great it's *going* to be! ENFPs are perhaps the most gifted type career-wise; they can do virtually anything they WANT to do.

An ENFP is Extraverted, iNtuitive, Feeling, & Perceiving

E— ENFPs are enthusiastic, open, outgoing, action-oriented **Extraverts**. People people. They are focused on the environment, constantly adapting to it, like chameleons. Everyone an ENFP knows, knows her as a different person. But almost all think she's great!

Ne— An ENFP *Extraverts* his **Dominant iNtuition** at you. That's what you hear most of the time— a stream-of-consciousness unending flow of thoughts and ideas, connected loosely at best. Often an abrupt change of subject is triggered by some minor event in the environment (which the ENFP has been scanning in the background while talking and 100% focused on you).

Fi— As a **Feeler**, an ENFP decides things, especially important things, with her **Auxiliary,** Feeling judgment, based on her own personal value system. It's usually people-oriented, and real-world based, since she's an Extravert.

However, in decision-making, ENFPs are Introverts. Their Feeling judgment is *Introverted*, so it requires time— quiet time— for processing. If an ENFP doesn't get *enough* Introversion time, he may not develop the Auxiliary function, Feeling, very well, may find deciding especially hard to do, and thus appear indecisive.

P— The ENFP is basically a **Perceiver**, more interested in information than decisions. ENFPs focus on more than one thing at a time, in a sort of parallel-processing mode that drives step-by-step people crazy. They are not naturally clean desk folks; their offices are notable for piles on every surface, including the floor. Because they live in the future, see so many possibilities, and make so many mental interconnections, they are reluctant to throw away even a piece of advertising mail that gives them an idea for a future project.

ENFPs are interruptible. In fact, they are a walking interruption. ENFPs are trying to do so many things at once that by the time they walk from the living room to the basement they forget what they went there for, because they got distracted by some other task they saw facing them there.

Te— ENFPs' **3rd Function, Thinking** judgment, is naturally **Extraverted**, and so gets called on to handle minor decisions with cool and effective logic. It may make the ENFP seem like an ENTP, since you see N and T. It can serve the ENFP well in analyzing and problem-solving; it provides convincing logical reasons for things the Feeling judgment has decided to do, or even improves the plan.

The "Shadow Side"—Si—Introverted Sensing is the ENFP's **4th function.** Not visible much to others, since it is internal, it's in fact largely unconscious. ENFPs aren't much tuned in to their 5 senses, but run on automatic pilot, iNtuitively. They may walk into a gap in the sidewalk (or avoid it) without consciously noticing it, where an observant Senser would see and avoid the danger. ENFPs have to develop little systems to keep track of things like their keys and wallets. Sensing is their last function to develop well, and a young Dominant iNtuitive of any type has to work especially hard to do Sensing tasks. Because it is Introverted, ENFPs' Sensing is best used in a quiet mode. When doing taxes, no distractions!

ENFPs are not well tuned in to their bodies. They tend to ignore all but the most blatant signals (really severe pain may get their attention) as they flow through the day. At night, when the lights go out and their iNtuitive scanners close down, the senses may get their turn. Then at last they may notice any ache or pain, or a bruise (they didn't notice the blow that caused it). When they do notice symptoms, they may not get around to seeing a doctor when they should, because so many other things demand attention.

ENFPs' 4th function Sensing can be a wonderfully helpful tool and a source of great spiritual insights when developed adequately. But it can get the ENFP in a lot of trouble if *not* developed. The fourth function is often the basis of "midlife crisis." Fourth function Sensing is often experienced as what Isabel Myers called "base sensuality." (Though it may seem quite enjoyable at the time!) The key is whether it is totally unconscious and controls the ENFP, and causes serious problems, or the ENFP is aware of and controls it. Best is for the ENFP to get lots of Sensing practice in safe situations, as in gardening, sports or other recreational activities, or in detail work like crewel. "Let the 4th function out to play," as they say, or it may break loose and damage your life!

NF— As NFs, ENFPs are the romantics, idealists, often writers, poets, composers, counselors. They are big on causes, usually global rather than local. They are susceptible to picking up guilt wherever they can find some, whether it's theirs, or deserved, or not. They may be constantly apologizing for the fact that it's raining today, as if they had caused it. Bump into an ENFP standing still, and he may apologize for being in your way (some types will call you a clumsy oaf!) Will Rogers ("I never met a man I didn't like") was probably an ENFP.

NP—As an NP, the ENFP, as we said, *Extraverts* iNtuition. But more, ENFPs are always focused on (positive) future possibilities, and they're the *opposite* of the detail-oriented SJ conservative who saves and watches every penny because hard times are coming, even if they aren't here yet. ENFPs are incurable optimists, but may be remiss in planning for the financial future, because things will be so wonderful soon and they'll have lots of money. ENFPs are big-picture people. Details drive them crazy, especially the need to spend long periods dealing with details. (They may do so, and successfully, however, if it is in service of their present Dream, whatever that may be.)

EF— ENFPs are Extraverts and warm Feelers. Though their Feeling function is internal, they show warmth powerfully with body language and tone of voice (which account for 93% of human communication). Both male and female ENFPs are often very physical, "huggy," sensual people.

FP— ENFPs are gentle FPs. Kindness is usually a built-in feature, along with concern for others, including animals. Because their Feeling is Introverted, they focus attention more on their mates and close loved ones than on friends and outsiders.

How to spot an ENFP
The first way to spot an ENFP is to *listen*— for that iNtuitive (NP) stream of consciousness. They pick up on a cue in a conversation, often a single word, and tell you what that *reminds* them of. Their conversation may be enthusiastic, upbeat, and cover 35 subjects in 10 minutes. There is much creativity, often wordplay.

ENFPs also tend to use a lot of non-specific words like "thingamajig" or "whatchamacallit." Their iNtuition is running too fast for their Sensing to provide the specific word.

Gender Differences— Female ENFPs are warm Feelers, Extraverted and creative. They have no problem fitting in with societal expectations for women— *if* they feel like it. Male ENFPs are Feelers in a Thinking milieu— but they Extravert their Thinking, and may develop it quite well as a result, so while they have a harder job early on, they may ultimately have an advantage over Thinkers whose Feeling has not been comparably developed. In some environments, ENFPs may even seem to operate as ENTJs if that is what the situation calls for.

By their nature, ENFPs do better, the higher they go in an organization. (They have assistants to handle Sensing details.) As bottom-level bean-counters, they may not survive.

ENFP Key Words

action	future-focused	visionary	tireless
enthusiastic	hate routine	caring	charismatic
exuberance	independent	gentle	charm
gregarious	individualistic	helpful	communicator
high energy	ingenuity	warm	dramatic
initiator	insightful	adventure	global
many friends	inspiration	flexible	mission
optimistic	inventive	fun	persuasive
people person	new skills	improvisation	seductive
results-oriented	non-conformist	impulse	self-expressive
big picture	original	interruptible	sensual
change	possibilities	non-judgmental	spread the word
creative	projects	playful	several things at once
eclectic	see meanings	procrastination	scan the environment
entrepreneur	variety	risk-taker	wing it!

ENFJ— Extraverted Feeler with Introverted iNtuition

Overview— An ENFJ is the friendliest, most charming, and charismatic of all 16 types. Because they seek and create harmony and are great communicators, ENFJs can be very effective leaders (and they tend to attract devoted followers).

Because they are Dominant Feelers, their time focus is on the past, where they have experienced good feelings before; they keep trying to recreate these positive experiences. Only 5% of the population are ENFJs, but they tend to be noticeable for their impact on society and their many friends.

An ENFJ is Extraverted, iNtuitive, Feeling and Judging.

E— ENFJs are outgoing, energetic and enthusiastic, action-oriented Extraverts, the consummate "people who like people." Relationships are at the center of their life. They think out loud, so they are great talkers, communicating constantly. It is not true that they account for 80% of phone company revenues, but they do contribute more than their share!

Ni— The ENFJ's **Auxiliary** or second-preferred function, **iNtuition**, is *Introverted.* They can be very creative, but need quiet, alone time to produce their best work. If they do not get *enough* alone time— a real possibility with popular ENFJs— they may not develop this creative side well, and adopt societal standards unexamined. ENFJs may try always to present themselves correctly, well-dressed (appropriately for the occasion). Most female ENFJs rarely go out without looking their best. They see possibilities in situations in terms of people: how particular people can be empowered and motivated to take control of their lives, succeed and be happy

Fe— ENFJs are **Dominant** *Extraverted* **Feelers**, which makes their constant communication especially warm, caring, and focused on whomever they are targeting at the moment. They have Feeling antennae out at all times, looking for similar Feeling energy in others. They are wonderfully supportive friends, stressing the good side at all times (The downside is, it may be difficult for them to criticize even when it's needed; and they may tend to take criticism too personally themselves.) They tend to value co-operation, though some (especially males) may have a competitive streak at times, as in sports.

They have great empathy for others, relating and even identifying with others' feelings at the deepest level. *Amicus est alter ego*— a friend is another self— is true of ENFJs. They may overidentify, and be in danger of merging; boundaries can be a problem for some ENFJs. This can lead to either their manipulating the other (ENFJs are skilled at this), or being victimized, taken advantage of, consciously or unconsciously, by the other(s)— sometimes many friends and organizations may try to monopolize the ENFJ to the point where there is little time left for self and family, or family members may do the same so there is little left for the ENFJ to build any part of her own life outside.

J— ENFJs are decisive, organized, orderly Judging types. They like things to be decided, or at least under control— their own, or someone else's, provided the other person knows what she is doing, especially in handling the people involved.

Se— ENFJs usually prefer to *Extravert* their **third function, Sensing**, to balance their Introverted iNtuition. So they may be seen as practical Sensing types, and indeed may make quite practical observations. But their deepest inner focus is on meaning, on possibilities, and they can be quite creative when they use their quiet iNtuitive side.

"Shadow Side" 4th Function Thinking—Ti— ENFJs *Introvert* their 4th function, **Thinking**, which is thus not given much opportunity to develop early in life, especially if the ENFJ is very Extraverted. There is a strong tendency to use Thinking selectively, choosing only arguments that support the ENFJ's Feeling judgment. The ENFJ's less developed 4th Function Thinking is likely to be expressed in "spurious conclusions," usually negative and aimed at the ENFJ himself. When in the grip of this shadow Thinking, ENFJs may appear and act, uncharacteristically, as cold as ice, even to those close to them. They will be especially sensitive to criticism aimed at this weaker side.

ENFJs at Midlife may tend to develop their more Introverted side, spending more time in quiet pursuits, and developing not only their creative Introverted iNtuition more impressively, but also developing a useful helper in their Introverted Thinking function, often ignored in the first half of their life.

NF— ENFJs are executive-type NFs— romantics who see possibilities for people; idealists who not only strive for their own ideals, but idealize the people they care most for and the causes they work for.

NJ— NJs are Creative Planners; they organize (J) the future(N). But this iNtuition is Introverted, and requires that the ENFJ spend enough Introverted time to develop it; otherwise the planning may be based on inadequate input.

EF— As Extraverts who are also Feelers, ENFJs are warm, and may be overtly seductive. ENFJs are Mentors, focusing on people to develop the best in them. They see themselves as reflected by others, so are especially sensitive to criticism. One zinger may outweigh a hundred compliments.

EJ— ENFJs are EJs— Extraverted Judgers— and focus on making decisions about the environment. They may seem especially decisive in organizational settings, though usually they are quite sensitive to others' feelings and needs. They can run a meeting with pleasant effectiveness, achieving the goal and sending everyone home happy. They have an uncanny ability to get the sense of the meeting, know what went on in terms of actual business, and how the relationships are working among the members.

FJ— The decisive function the world sees is Feeling, and ENFJs are known for expressing Feelings and Feeling judgments as a major part of their communication. It's one part of how we identify an ENFJ— the warm positive enthusiastic Feeling judgments:"Wonderful!!" But sometimes their judgments can be negative, even ice cold. When they want to attack, they know perfectly what hot buttons to push. This usually occurs only if someone has been unkind, or thoughtless, or hurt the feelings of someone dear to the ENFJ.

ENFJ Life Themes—Relationships with people are a key, if not *the* key focus of ENFJs. Their aim for life is to find or create warm feeling-connections with other people. Though they may rise to lead (or create) a large organization, it is the individual people-contacts that bring joy to their lives. Harmony is a goal and an expectation; but this is in frequent conflict with a desire to repress, deny or even, perhaps unconsciously, be dishonest about things that are not harmonious. They may spend so much time and energy taking care of and nurturing others, that they ignore or repress their own needs. They themselves need the kind of strokes they give so freely, and they need a chance to share their pain.

How to Spot ENFJs— ENFJs can radiate friendliness from across a room. They tend to be dressed appropriately for whatever the occasion. In conversation they spout (usually very positive) Feeling judgments. Everything is wonderful, special, exciting, delicious, *the very best* (whatever) *I've ever seen!* You can hear the exclamation points! There may be a phone glued to one ear. They are busy calling people to make them (and themselves) feel good, or at least better.

Gender Differences— ENFJ males are warm and friendly, but being socialized as males may be more competitive. Female ENFJs reflect much of what we call "feminine," and will have a wide circle of supportive friends, female and male.

ENFJ Key Words:

charisma	empathetic	vulnerable
influential	feeling-seekers	warmth, nurture
lead parties	hard time saying "No."	decisive
manipulative	harmonious	like things settled
persuasive	ideals, idealizing	planful
restless at times	long for the perfect	guilt
communicators	may impose own values	motivators
enthusiasm	praisers, complimenters	seductive
great speakers	relationships	conscientious
outgoing, friendly	sensitive	expectant
talkers	socially adept	people organizers
vision, insight	tactful	black-and-white thinking
compassionate	take criticism personally	may jump to conclusion
concentrate on one's	try to please	natural leader
admirable qualities	value-driven	organize groups
denial	victimizable	

INTJ—Introverted iNtuitive with Extraverted Thinking

Overview— INTJs are blessed with a powerful internal possibility mill that is constantly generating new ideas, improvements in the status quo, a constantly polished vision of what could be. They are usually committed to getting the world to match this vision, and will not easily give up on it. Supremely independent, perhaps more than any other Type, they may well keep this inner vision and process to themselves, and report out only logical and often critical conclusions. As Thinkers, they see time as a linear flow from past-to-present-to-future. As Dominant iNtuitors, their time focus is really on the future.

INTJs are Introverted, iNtuitive, Thinking and Judging—Introverted iNtuitives, who when they deal with the outer world prefer to use their logical Thinking function.

I— INTJs' prefer **Introversion**, though their upbringing will have an effect on this. Their intellectual abilities may tend to isolate them in school; or it may win them positive attention and draw them comfortably out of their shell. But they will always need quiet time to "charge their batteries." They may seem distant, especially when they are going over things in their minds. They are likely to prefer one-on-one conversations, and have a small number of close friends rather than the Extravert's easy familiarity with many. Small talk is not for them; they prefer in-depth knowledge of a subject and tend to be specialists rather than generalists. INTJs are likely to value control, both control of themselves and often of others. They are not usually excitable, except perhaps in an area where they are very heavily invested; even with a major aspect of their vision, they are likely to show controlled enthusiasm.

Ni— **iNtuition** is the **Dominant**, keystone of an INTJ's personality, the Captain of the ship; but it is usually **Introverted**, and only a few very close friends get to see it up close. Much time is spent in developing and considering alternative possibilities, after which the INTJ reports out a logical conclusion as to what to do. We never know the wild and varied ideas they have constructed and discarded; but we are impressed with the creativity and complexity of the plan they finally propose— or "announce," as the case may be! iNtuition is the source of their vision, the plan for the future that drives the INTJ's life. Their iNtuition allows incredible complexity and comfort with seeming paradox, which will all be resolved in the future perfect— the time frame in which they spend most waking hours. It brings them unbidden a stream of new ways to improve everything in sight, and even to improve some things that exist only in their own complicated minds.

Te— Extraverted Thinking judgment is the **Auxiliary**, second-in-command through which the INTJ communicates with the outside world when necessary. It announces rational decisions and the logical support for them. It may be, especially with younger INTJs or those whose other side has not yet been well developed, a bit curt and critical. It challenges others' ideas, heedless of the rank or authority of the person proposing them, whenever they need correction, improvement, or replacement. The Thinking function is usually tough-minded and impersonal. This can get INTJs in trouble with Feelers who may take criticism personally, even if intended constructively. But it can also save the day when it detects a flaw that might otherwise have been disastrous.

J— As **Judgers** or Deciders, INTJs like to get things settled, preferably early. They plan ahead masterfully, break things down into component parts, operate in an organized fashion, and try to avoid stressful last-minute crises.

Fi— The INTJ's **3rd function, Feeling** judgment, is **Introverted**, which makes them a romantic NF inside. But rarely do you see that aspect of their nature. Introverted Feeling is slow to be expressed (or even identified), but it can be very loyal to those closest to the INTJ. It is not "wasted" on casual acquaintances, who see only the practical and logical side, and may never suspect the warmth that lies beneath the surface. Still, INTJs are Thinkers, and in a clash between head and heart, the head is likely to win.

"Shadow Side" 4th Function Sensing— INTJs' weakest and least developed function is **Extraverted Sensing**. They aim it at the outer world, may develop specific areas of Sensing expertise, and may be quite sensitive to criticism around it; but it will never be the equal of the iNtuition they keep facing inside. It is important for INTJs to develop this Sensing, perhaps by letting it out to play from time to time, in sports, hobbies, or other hands-on activities. If not developed, it can be a problem at midlife when it demands attention, perhaps in inappropriate attractions and what Isabel Myers called "base sensuality." At its best, an INTJ's Sensing can be a real help, providing deep spiritual insights or allowing the INTJ to perform lengthy detailed analyses or operations if that will serve the vision of the iNtuition.

NT— In Temperament terms, INTJs are NTs—iNtuitive Thinkers, creative and logical, which makes them great scientists and inventors, systems people who understand (they *need* to understand!) *how* things work, and *why* things happen. NT children always ask, "Why, Daddy?" Grownup NTs ask the same question. NTs often seek knowledge for its own sake, though they are also good at applying it to their advantage.

NJ— NJs are decisive **Judgers**, who prefer to Introvert their creative **iNtuitive** function (they need quiet time to dream up ideas) and show the world their practical Sensing side— less preferred, but Extraverted so it shows. They may get a vision— see some creative future possibility that they want to pursue, realistic or not— and then try to sell you on it with all the practical facts their Sensing side can uncover. As Js they *will* have an agenda, and introverting N, it will be creative, and often not made public until the best possible time, if ever.

IJ— As **Introverts** and **Judgers**, they may be quiet, controlled, and show minimum facial affect except when speaking about something specific where it would be appropriate. They may tend to expect you to mindread their thoughts and moods; this can be hard if they are in a happy place but wearing a face that gives no hint of it. Thinkers are even more likely than Feeling types to wear this mask of inscrutability.

TJ— The **Thinking-Judging** combination is often found among executives, and INTJs are some of the best— often found at the head of an entrepreneurial enterprise that they started themselves, as well as high up in large organizations. The make decisions easily, and they tend to be logical decisions. What could be better than that?

INTJ Life Themes— It is INTJs' very nature to strive for excellence. They respect knowledge and education, have a high tolerance for complexity and theory— but appreciate what works. They are always improving things, people, or systems. Most important of all, a deep inner vision brings them a sense of mission and meaning, and guides all they do.

How to Spot INTJs— INTJs are often taciturn, but not stern. They often have a great smile, but do not use it perhaps enough. Their speech is usually brief, logical, objective, often Thinking judgments— logical conclusions about something. When they speak, it is usually polished and well organized, frequently technical, with "75¢ words." Many INTJs are scientists. They know the jargon of their profession and have extensive vocabularies and assume others do, too. Listen for words like "I think," not "I feel." Many tend to be visual and will draw you a map rather than give you step-by step directions. Competence, excellence, organization is in all they undertake, or they will not undertake it. Small talk is a turnoff to most INTJs, unless they are doing research on small talk.

Gender Differences— INTJ women have the double difficulty of dealing with being a rare 1% type in general, plus learning how to be a woman who prefers Thinking to Feeling judgment. This puts her in potential conflict with her peers, teachers, and often parents' expectations, as well as what society is telling her about women and little girls every day. Some may become social misfits but professional successes. Most develop their Feeling function quite competently so as to fulfil their role as women as seen by society, and this gives them an advantage over many Feeling women (who do not receive similar encouragement to develop their Thinking side) and Thinking men (who do not get their Feeling side so well developed until much later, if they are lucky).

INTJ men have to deal with being "different," as 1% types. Their interests are often at odds with those of their peers, even though they be Thinkers. INTJs are often "late bloomers." Many come into their own after they find their way into an environment that fits; others adapt their natural style to excel in whatever environment in which they find themselves.

INTJ Key Words

privacy	self-improvement	insensitive	order
big picture	symbolic	principles	planful
complexity	argumentative	skeptical	can seem arrogant
improvements	can seem cold	control	plans
independent	challenge	decisive	strategies
inner vision(s)	critical	disciplined	systems
possibilities	impersonal	like things settled	theoretical models

---

INTP—Introverted Thinkers with Extraverted iNtuition

Overview— INTPs are quiet logical theoreticians— but you may rarely see that most important side of them except through the output it produces. Great respecters of learning for learning's sake, they can concentrate (perhaps better than any Type) in order to comprehend with the perfect clarity that is their goal and analyze experiences, things, situations, even people, for patterns, categories and insights to understanding the systems and concepts involved. They wish to develop their own philosophical system of how the world works, several blanket premises that direct their lives. As Jung's disciple Van der Hoop puts it, they make "endless preparations for life," even in little matters, before taking any action. As Dominant Thinkers their time focus is a logical linear past-to-present-to-future flow. They basically live today, using the experience of the past to plan for the future.

INTPs are Introverted, iNtuitive, Thinking and Perceiving— Introverted Thinkers, who when they deal with the outer world prefer to use their creative iNtuitive function.

I— INTPs have the **Introvert's** need for quiet alone time to do their best work, to access their Dominant function, Thinking, and to recharge their batteries after they have been dealing with people in the "outer world." They are generally not gregarious chatters, and tend to polish what they need to communicate before they speak. So the speech you hear is often terse, pithy, even deep in its thought content. It can also be a persona, to conceal the real person from the world.

Ne— When **Extraverting**, INTPs prefer to use their second-best, "Auxiliary" function, **iNtuition.** They can get going on a stream of consciousness that leaps from point to point or from observation to conclusion, often with no visible means of connection save in their mind.

Ti— **Introverted Thinking** is the Dominant, most important part of the INTP's makeup; but it's generally kept inside, concentrating, planning the operations, classifying, analyzing, planning, critiquing and deciding while, if necessary, the #2 iNtuition is out there keeping the world at bay. People may seem like an unwelcome intrusion when the INTP is really concentrating on some important new concept. While we see INTPs as laid back, they are Dominant Thinkers and are judging and critiquing everything internally.

P— **Perceivers—** Though INTPs may have a perfectionist streak, especially for their own output, generally they are flexible, casual, sometimes too much so; deadlines can be a problem, and some of their many projects, once fascinating, may not get finished. But their casual Perceptive Attitude is partly balanced by Introversion and Thinking discipline.

As Perceptives they want to be prepared, and may work and rework all the details in advance, taking no action until they have the perfect Plan. At which point, they may not feel much need to take the action at all, since the perfect outcome is already assured; the pleasure was in the planning!

Si— An INTP's **3rd function Introverted Sensing** doesn't show up in the INTP 4-letter Type, but is important for the facts it feeds to the Thinking process. There is a tendency to give facts short shrift; but the INTP must learn to check them out carefully and accurately or they may torpedo the logical Plan.

The exact opposite of the ESFJ "hostess with the mostes'," INTPs may be the Type most socially disadvantaged. Though as always there are notable exceptions where they have worked hard at competence in this area, some have a tendency to belittle such socializing.

"Shadow Side" 4th Function — Fe— Extraverted Feeling is the least-preferred, 4th function for an INTP. It can be the source of great insights and great joy, and the cause of much trouble, particularly at midlife, if it is not allowed expression from time to time. As an Extraverted function, it is visible to others when it is used; but it tends not to be used often. It can give the INTP consternation because it is by definition not logical. And since it is largely unconscious, it crops up unexpectedly at the worst possible times to embarrass and confuse. It can cause powerful feelings of love, often for a totally inappropriate person; the more inappropriate, the more likely the urge is really about the INTP's own development, not the person projected onto. At its best, this function can also be the source of great spiritual insight; it may also help the Thinker develop great effectiveness in dealing with people.

NT— INTPs are "NTs" by Temperament, wanting to have the power of knowledge over the universe. They are systems people, seeing, understanding, or designing new or improved systems for whatever interests them. They are interested in learning, especially matters scientific, technical, mathematical or philosophical. INTPs' knowledge is seldom superficial. Their judgments are objective; but since the input source is iNtuition, it is paradoxically not always clear how they arrived at them, and they may sometimes have trouble defending their positions— which are nonetheless firmly held. INTPs may, however, be more tolerant of differing views than many Types, accepting paradox, and looking at everything including their own position with skepticism. (INTPs are great skeptics.)

NP— Their interests are likely to be eclectic. As **iNtuitive Perceivers**, they stumble into all manner of subjects, and manage to see connections to whatever else they have been dealing with— connections few others would see, even after it is pointed out to them. Their iNtuition can bring a considerable reputation for creativity, especially when they monitor it with their strong Thinking (even more so when they have available a Senser to help bring their ideas into fruition).

IP— INTPs like to get all the information they can, examine it for patterns and possible hypotheses, and eventually abstract it into a coherent whole and draw conclusions— all the while continuing to add more information, and fitting that in somehow. They start with their own premise, preferring deductive reasoning to inductive.

IN— Good at teaching complex subjects, INTPs are chiefly found at college level; few are interested in working with small children or uncomplicated topics.

In love, INTPs more than other Types can feel awkward and ill at ease. They may preplan every detail of an expected encounter in advance, for better or for worse, depending on whether things go according to plan. They can be quite sensitive in such a situation, though this is often denied.

INTP Life Themes— INTPs are great systematizers, architects of ideas, as Keirsey put it, in whatever subject. They go for the basic constructs, learn, understand, and improve on them. They love to create new ideas and let someone else carry out the details of the project. They set high standards for others (higher for themselves). When another is intellectually slower, they have to work at being patient.

INTPs are likely to be devoted spouses, but spend much time in their heads or on their projects, and may miss birthdays and little cues that the mate needs attention. (If your mate is an INTP, ask for what you need!)

How to Spot INTPs— Often found in or around university settings, species INTP appreciates higher learning and intelligence in general. They desire to learn all they can about the world in general, and about the specific specialties that interest them (often more than one, in sequence; even Einstein, a classic INTP, moved from physics to philosophy and music). They polish their thinking and often their speaking to precise perfection; everything must fit, the exact word must be selected. They have little respect for authority per se, only for that which an individual has earned by his or her own qualifications. Classic out-of-the-box thinkers, they are creative and may enjoy being iconoclastic.

Gender Differences— As Dominant Thinking Types, INTPs are especially subject to sex /gender differences. Female INTPs may feel particularly alone and disconnected from their classmates. It helps if their parents and teachers can provide support for their natural preferences, while assisting them to join in the activities (e.g., athletics) that may not naturally appeal to them, so they can find peer acceptance and self esteem early in life. Otherwise, they may get to college before they find many others like themselves and are able to feel OK about their nature and others'.

Male INTPs also may not find school a joyful experience, because their intellectual interests and the rarity of their Type may be isolating. As adults, they may be late bloomers if they have not developed enough Extraversion to be comfortable in social interactions. But competence in work often provides the necessary self-assurance.

INTP Key Words

abstraction	synthesizing	skeptical	systems
calm	clarity	flexible	theoretical
concentration	concepts	classification	understanding
reflective	logic	competence	curiosity
complexity	objectivity	intellectual	open-minded
creative	precision	preplanning	internal order
possibilities	principles	self-mastery	obstinate

ENTP—Extraverted iNtuitive with Introverted Thinking

Overview—ENTPs are enthusiastic followers of their own creative inspirations, and they are expert at getting others to buy into those visions. They do not have a single career track, but usually a variety of often wildly varied occupations over the years; these reflect a succession of new visions and interests that each caught the iNtuition of the ENTP. As Dominant iNtuitives their time focus is the future; they may not notice much detail of what's going on now.

ENTPs are Extraverted, iNtuitive, Thinking and Perceiving— Extraverted iNtuitives, who when they make decisions prefer to use their Introverted logical Thinking function.

E— ENTPs focus their creativity on the outer world of real people, places and things; how they work, how they relate, how they can be improved. ENTPs tend to have high energy levels, particularly when they are enthusiastically engaged in a project of importance to them. They are initiators, action people, friendly and gregarious, preferring to work with other people rather than alone. They like literally to think out loud; this is usually a flow of iNtuitive ideas, of which they are first aware when they hear themselves say them.

Ne— The **Dominant** function for an ENTP is **Extraverted iNtuition**—the creative source that provides an unstoppable flow of ideas and ingenious ways of solving problems. ENTPs are intellectually focused, appreciate learning for the sake of learning, enjoy theory, symbolism, abstractions and complexity. They like to apply all this, however, to find creative solutions to real-world physical situations and relationship problems. These ideas form the vision that infuses everything the ENTP does. They are future-focused, long-term, big-picture people. They do not see so much what is there, as what *could* be there; not the literal words, but what is between the lines.

Ti— ENTPs make their important decisions logically, analytically, impersonally, using their **Auxiliary Introverted Thinking** function. This means they must shut down and find quiet concentration time to decide, since this part of them is effectively an Introvert. The Thinking preference makes ENTPs tough-minded, able to find the flaws in something—which can sound critical to a Feeler, who may take criticism personally. (ENTPs have trouble even imagining how important this is to Feelers.) ENTPs are skeptics, "show me" people. They love a good argument, and often take the opposite side

208

just for the fun of it. Great debaters, they ask tough, impressively probing questions. Especially of themselves; this Thinking facing inward makes them their own toughest critics.

P— As **Perceivers**, ENTPs are spontaneous and flexible, easy-going people. Supremely interruptible, they often get into last-minute situations— which is where they do their best work. In fact, it often takes the pressure of a deadline to get them moving toward completion of a project. Where Judgers need plans, ENTPs often leap in without more than a vague iNtuitive impression of what they will do, and develop their strategy pragmatically as they go along.

Fe— ENTPs may be mistaken for ENFPs at times because they **Extravert** their **3rd function Feeling** function; and their Extraversion also gives them an easy connection with people. They may decide a minor matter with the Feeling function, especially when in an Extraverted mode. But when they have a chance to Introvert on it, they may reverse the decision, giving the Thinking judgment precedence. And major decisions are usually made by Thinking, not Feeling judgment, though this can often surprise Feelers who heard Feeling words and perceived real warmth, and were unprepared for a cool impersonal judgment.

ENTPs' Extraverted Feeling is likely to focus more on the new casual acquaintance than on the loyal long-term relationship, which may be taken for granted, or come to seem tiresome. With this external Feeling, but with Thinking making the final decision, ENTPs may get a reputation for "using" people, especially if they switch from F to T too quickly. Never mind that it's as much the other's expectations as the ENTP's leading them on; it's good to watch out for it.

"Shadow Side" 4th Function for ENTPs is **Introverted Sensing**, which often comes onstream full force at "midlife crisis," especially if it has not had adequate opportunity to come out and play over the years. NTs in particular may be liable to suppress their weakest function precisely because it is least developed, and they have a need to be and appear competent at all times. Details trip them up and drive them crazy; and the unexpected power of sensuality can overwhelm an ENTP who has been focused too heavily on the intellectual and ignored the Sensing function.

NT— The NT Temperament means ENTPs are charged with what Keirsey describes as a Promethean need for competence, for knowledge and power over nature. They want to be able to understand, to know how to do, *everything*, even if they do not actually need to do it. They are energized by a new idea or concept, and how to apply it to their world.

NP— As i**Ntuitive Perceivers,** they get their primary information input intuitively, through mental connections with other seemingly unrelated material already in their memory banks. Verbally, they often respond to your statement with a comment based on what in their experience it reminds them of. This may be helpful, or it may feel to you as if they are switching the subject from you to them. It is simply the way their minds work first, thinking aloud, in a "stream of consciousness."

EP— Extraverted Perceivers, ENTPs are interested in information on the real world. Comfortable with the environment, they move in it flexibly, casually and expressively.

TP— We discussed the Introverted Thinking function earlier under the Auxiliary topic. Thinking Perceivers in general show the world a warm Feeling face, but make tough Thinking decisions when they have time to close down and Introvert on the matter.

ENTP Life Themes— ENTPs' lives are often a book of many diverse chapters. They always have a cluster of projects in process, starting more than they (or any human) can finish in a single lifetime. Many of these will be about improving things or solving problems. They may be entrepreneurial ventures, or at least entrepreneurial in spirit. Often in later life when the Sensing function has developed well enough to be a real assistant (or at least less of a stumbling block), they will find things come more easily to them, though the ENTP's gifts may well achieve early success on the sheer power of their creativity and ability to deal flexibly and logically with the environment.

How to Spot ENTPs— The first clue is Extraversion, of course. As Extraverts, ENTPs provide you with more clues than Introverts do. And what you hear Extraverted is iNtuition— the stream-of-consciousness flow of ideas, connections, instant reactions, often puns or wordplay. So far, we have identified EN—P. The T vs. F is harder to spot, because the ENTP extraverts F, and the ENFP extraverts T. Here Temperament is helpful; is this an NT scientist-type, focused on competence and sometimes one-up-manship— or a warm-fuzzies romantic NF? In many cases it is difficult for the EN—P himself to decide; don't be upset if you are not sure about someone else!

Gender Differences— As Thinkers, ENTP women are likely to be swimming upstream much of the time. But as women, they are likely to be strongly socialized to act the Feeler's role, and develop this side of themselves much more than do most ENTP males. ENTPs naturally Extravert their Feeling function; and as Extraverts they spend much time Extraverting, so their Feeling may be quite well developed.

ENTP males are Thinkers in a male Thinker milieu, and though they Extravert Feeling, this will usually be less encouraged and so less developed.

ENTP Key Words

action	inspiration	objective	eternal learning
enthusiastic	inventive	adaptability	intellectual
exuberance	new skills	adventure	one-up-manship
results-oriented	nonconformity	fun	scientific
big picture	original	improvisation	systems thinking
change	possibilities	impulse	challenge
creativity	variety	interruptible	charm
entrepreneur	visionary	non-judgmental	communicator
experimenter	wing it!	procrastination	mission
hate routine	analyst	risk-taker	objective
independent	argumentative	tireless	projects
individualistic	debating	competence	
ingenuity	logical	competitive	

© 1994 William DG Murray PO Box 200 Gladwyne PA 19035-0200 USA

ENTJ—Extraverted Thinkers with Introverted iNtuition

Overview— ENTJs are sometimes called the "Field Marshall" Type. They like control and tend to take charge if given half a chance. They are often hearty, enthusiastic, friendly— but businesslike, not given to rambling on too long. Driven by logic, they can make tough decisions, but may be seen as not very warm by Feeling Types. As Dominant Thinkers their time focus is a logical linear past-to-present-to-future flow. They use the experience of the past to plan for the future. As iNtuitives, they focus more on future planning than present enjoyment.

ENTJs are Extraverted, iNtuitive, Thinking and Judging— Extraverted Thinkers, who when they deal with the inner world prefer to use their creative iNtuitive function.

E— As **Extraverts**, ENTJs are action people, often take-charge folks who want to steer the boat themselves, in the direction they think best. They are comfortable and generally self-confident in the external world.

Ni— **iNtuition**, the ENTJ's source of information, and **Auxiliary** or second-preferred function, is **Introverted**, so ENTJs tend to develop their best ideas alone, not by brainstorming. They deal well with complexity and interrelationships, and make good systems people. They constantly improve the system. If things get too routine, they may get bored and demotivated quickly. Change and variety energize them— new worlds to conquer.

Te— **Thinking**, the **Dominant** function for the ENTJ, is **Extraverted**. So that's what you hear from them most of the time: logical Thinking judgments, usually brief, clear, and seldom repetitively stated. Sometimes this means "Here's why your precious idea won't work," with little recognition that this will have emotional impact on the listener. ENTJs often love a good argument (they are perhaps the quintessential prosecuting attorney), and their competitive nature likes nothing better than winning; but if you beat them fairly, they will have great respect for you.

Supremely rational, they are reason-driven. Give them a *logical* reason if you want their support; not a value-based Feeling reason. They develop a systematic logical view of the world, and try to fit everything into it. Anything that does not fit requires redoing the scheme (a major undertaking) or is discarded as illogical. This habit helps them express things— including their iNtuitive vision— with great clarity.

212

J— ENTJs are decisive **Judgers**— sometimes too decisive, when they act before getting enough information. They want to get things decided, now if not sooner. They can tend to make decisions for everyone in the family— or at least spell out the basic system under which it operates.

They are future-planners and organizers. They analyze problems, develop solutions, and schedule the steps to be taken, even in day-to-day family matters.

Se— **Sensing**, their **3rd function**, does not show up in the ENTJ 4-letter Type, but it is of course there, and is **Extraverted**, so you may see more of the Sensing function (facts) than of the preferred iNtuition, which is used chiefly internally. To others, ENTJs can look like ESTJs, since ENTJs extravert S and T. (ESTJs, conversely, extravert N and T.)

"Shadow Side" 4th Function — Fi— The "Achilles' heel and pearl of great price," as Terence Duniho put it, is the ENTJ's fourth function **Introverted Feeling**. It can get them into great trouble and distress ("A feeling! How embarrassing!"). It can also lead them to greater understanding of self and others, and therefore greater effectiveness, and much joy in loving relationships. Being Introverted, it is not usually visible to others; and being the fourth function, it is largely unconscious, and not readily accessible to the ENTJ. It takes *time* for ENTJs to get in touch with a Feeling judgment, even if they want to (sometimes they don't). Often their body language gives away their feelings and even their Feeling judgments to others long before the ENTJ is aware of them. It is best to allow time and find safe occasions to express this function, so that it does not blindside you at the worst possible time!

NT— As NTs, ENTJs pursue knowledge for its own sake, using it to perfect their systematic worldview. They may seek shortcuts in this process, to let them get on with their Extraverted life. One such is to learn and adopt a system that makes sense, that was developed by an authority with appropriate credentials (NTs always require proper credentials, or they discount or ignore the input). If Feelers live by their values, ENTJs live, at least consciously, by their principles. Like the Feelers, usually they expect you to do so, too.

NJ— As NJs, ENTJs are creative, but do their best creative work in quiet private time, with the door shut, or while taking a walk. Then they will sell their creative results to you with the powerful logic of their Extraverted Thinking. They develop these ideas in support of their Dominant Thinking, which they use to analyze and organize and systematize the product before they present it. It is a powerful combination.

EJ— Extraverted Judgers make decisions about the environment, and they usually make them quickly. Often *too* quickly, without adequate input; but they adjust quickly, also, learning by trial and error. They tend to get the boat away from the dock first, then check the charts for direction. (Perceivers may wait until the whole course is charted, and miss the tide.) ENTJs speak in judgments, decisions. It sounds as if everything is already cast in bronze, and no disagreement will be tolerated. Not so; often they are thinking out loud, and their tentative judgment is being expressed. It only *sounds* unarguable. They usually appreciate a challenge that objectively improves the idea. (They may still see the result as their idea, even if it ends up 98% your idea and 2% theirs.) And they have expectations, in any situation; better live up to them!

TJ— ENTJs are what Keirsey calls the commandants. A bright ENTJ is perhaps the most formidable of the four TJ types (who are to be found running almost any organization of significant size). They spout irrefragable logic and can seem to brook no disagreement. Certainly they are the most self-confident of the Types (though even they have moments of self-doubt, they can usually dismiss these as illogical).

ENTJ Life Themes— Control is a key ENTJ theme. They like to be in control, and they may fear when someone else is. As a result, ENTJs often end up in leadership roles.

Objective principles are another key theme for ENTJs— the system (or systems— they may have several for different aspects of life) under whose principles they operate. This is not always apparent to others, but it is the internal structure under which the ENTJ functions.

ENTJs are quick, confident, decisive. Decisions, based on their principles, are often immediately obvious to them.

Human relationships can be an area where the ENTJ has difficulty, at home or at work. People who function based on their Feeling values may not buy into the ENTJ's logical Thinking decisions, with resultant labor unrest or family conflict. As ENTJs mature and develop their softer side, they will find they have magically become more effective.

How to Spot ENTJs— ENTJs are Extraverts, but they may not be screaming Extraverts. They are enthusiastic, and tend to talk and move quickly. Very quickly. They are not patient with long explanations, and want you to get to the point, especially if they are in charge. And they often are. They are assertive, can be domineering, but hard workers with extremely high standards, most of all for themselves. They can drive themselves to an early workaholic death unless they moderate these tendencies.

Gender Differences— ENTJ commandant males fit the male stereotype. The problem is, so do most female ENTJs. A tough take-charge woman who steps on toes and doesn't realize it can have real problems being accepted, either by men or by other women. Though some ENTJ women are well socialized by family and society to develop their Feeling function more in line with the softer "feminine" approach, this is not easy or usual.

ENTJ Key Words		
empirical	reason	confident
energy	closure	demanding
hearty	control	efficiency
quick	decisions	intellectual
change-oriented	goals	visual
possibilities	orderly	aggressive
vision	organizing	command
argumentative	planning	competitive
confrontive	structure	take-charge
critical	challenge	impatient
objectivity	competence	urgency

Chapter 8

The Shadow Knows

No discussion of Type is complete without mentioning the "shadow side," or (to avoid confusion with Jungians for whom that term "shadow" has a specific meaning), the "shadow *function*," i.e., the 4th or least-preferred of your four functions (Sensing, Intuition, Thinking, & Feeling). The least-preferred is always the opposite of the most preferred, i.e., if we prefer Feeling most, our 4th function will be Thinking, and vice versa; if we prefer iNtuition our 4th is Sensing; and iNtuition is the 4th function for Dominant Sensers.

Let's look at *4th function Sensing*— the way it operates for a *Dominant iNtuitive*. If a Dominant Senser is attentive to detail, the iNtuitive using 4th function Sensing can be the most nit-picking detail-monger imaginable! Things of that sort, when done at last, are likely to be overdone quite badly. The worst nitpicker of all is the guy who can't stand nitpickers! So he carries it to extremes. That negative which we identify most easily in others is usually the part of ourselves which is least preferred, least developed, and so least used and most likely to be unreliable and/or get us in trouble. We may commonly repress that aspect of ourselves, or try to. We may even succeed for a time, but we have a serious need to use our fourth function (all functions, of course). The fourth is largely unconscious, so if we do not develop it, we can be blindsided when it suddenly kicks in and takes over, causing us to do something we

216

would not normally have done. (Sometimes to our extreme embarrassment!) Afterwards we may say, "That *can't* have been me!"

BEFORE BURNING

   THESE PAPERS,

     LET ME
    MAKE SURE
  THEY'RE IN

ALPHABETICAL ORDER.

Ashleigh Brilliant

© *Ashleigh Brilliant 1969*   *Pot-Shots No 116*

That's what the iNtuitive here did: he's using his 4th Function Sensing, all right— to put the papers in alphabetical order— but the whole task could be skipped in this case! (Of course, he's exercising his fourth function, and at least won't do any damage if he makes a few mistakes!)

On the subject of the 4th Function, a few important points:

1. *There is a real and absolute need for everyone to develop the fourth function* (whichever that may be for them) through use in appropriate situations (see Table on page 218). Otherwise as we grow older, it will still be quite immature, and be likely to pop out and get us in trouble when we least expect or can least afford it. An example of a Dominant iNtuitor's shadow Sensing is what Isabel Myers calls "base sensuality." Often at midlife, developing fourth function Sensing shows up as powerful sexual urges, often toward someone inappropriate or unavailable. Nearly everybody *has* these urges; the key is to be aware of them, recognize them and the *message* they are delivering in regard to our need to develop the fourth function. (We do not need to *act* on the urges any more than we need to kill the umpire when we feel like it. But many people *do* act on these midlife urges, causing much upset in their lives and

217

If You Are a Dominant:	Your 4th Function Is:	How Shadow Side Is Experienced/ Shows As:	Dangers/Consequences of Acting On Shadow's Direction:
N	S	"Base sensuality;" appeal of senses, inappropriate/ uncontrolled indulgence, e.g., sex, overeating.	May have unwise affair, risk marriage, family relationships; may get obese, cause medical problems, shorten life, increase insurance cost.
S	N	Perceive future unrealistically (positively or negatively— usually as disaster about to strike); "doom & gloom."	May be depressed, expecting worst — may not see best alternative courses of action; may be paralyzed by indecision or choose lesser of two evils, when good was also a choice, but not perceived; may overinsure against unlikely risk; take precipitous action in preparation for expected disaster, sell out at bottom of market.
F	T	"Spurious conclusions," usually negative, about self, one's competence, desirability, goodness or worth. Based on faulty logic, overgeneralization.	Depression, self-denigration, poor decisions based on faulty logic.
T	F	*Very* strong feelings - e.g., love for another (often inappropriate) person; anger or feelings of hate that may lead to explosive acting out, spouse beating, or worse.	Uncontrolled rages, even physical violence; inappropriate love affairs.

218

What To Do Immediately When In the Grip of the Shadow *(Revert to strength: Try using Your Dominant in its preferred direction)*	How to Develop Your 4th Function Healthily Long-Term *(Use your 4th function in "safe" recreational situations.)*
Brainstorm—ideas, things you'd like to do, places you'd like to go, people you'd like to do things with; plan some great future event; read something that interests you, and tell someone about the new ideas you had while reading.	Massage; hands-on hobbies (e.g., woodworking, crewel, gardening); taxes, accounting, figure your net worth, do a family budget; travel, art (focusing on Sensing: study details of the work). Focus on the present.
Go work in garden, do hands-on hobbies (e.g., woodworking, crewel, gardening); taxes, accounting, figure your net worth, do a family budget; travel, art (focusing on Sensing: study details of the work).	Do puzzles, wordplay, write a poem, brainstorm ideas on something fun. Work on the "vision thing." List future goals/things you'd like to do/see/have/be if anything were possible.
Make someone happy. Get into own Feeling side: nostalgia of good past times. Express your own good positive feelings toward/about someone or some situation.	Study math or logic. Do puzzles and thinking games. Think about all consequences of something you'd like to do -- construct scenarios of how things might work out. Play bridge.
Get back to rationality. Ask yourself who, what, when, why about the situation. Analyze and quantify what you can. Count to ten (or higher if needed), but *postpone* action; sleep on it. Change the subject.	Play Feeling games; pet your dog or cat; play gently with a child (let them win). Be childlike (in a safe space).

those around them.) A Dominant Thinker's 4th function Feeling can cause very similar love attachments to highly inappropriate individuals— in effect, the same result, for slightly different reasons.

2. Healthy ways to develop the fourth function include *recreational* use of it. Since our fourth is least developed and least expert, we feel uncomfortable when important stakes are riding on it. We can't afford to look less than expert. Recreational applications are more casual; we don't have to win every game. We may even get better and better, and watch our scores improve to the point of acceptability. Besides sports, recreational uses of Sensing include gardening, woodworking, crewel, petting your dog or cat, and of course sex, preferably in situations that will not cause trouble! (We don't mean this book to be an intellectual excuse for midlife crisis affairs, though it may well provide an explanation after the fact. Consider it a warning so you can inoculate yourself before the disease hits, and develop antibodies when it strikes.)

3. The fourth function is not only a source of potential trouble, but also of potential spiritual depth and great insight.* You can develop your fourth function to the point of adequacy, so it can help you when you need it.

 * See "Your Shadow Side: the Fourth Function— Achilles' Heel and Pearl of Great Price," by Terence Duniho, Type & Temperament Press 1992.

ALWAYS
TAKE
YOUR
VITAMINS
IN ALPHABETICAL ORDER:

IT HASN'T YET
BEEN PROVEN NECESSARY,
BUT WHY TAKE CHANCES?

© Ashleigh Brilliant 1982   Pot-Shots No 2655

The Pot-Shot® at left combines the above fourth function Sensing problem with an iNtuitive's tendency to act on non-facts, on unproven possibilities, assumptions or superstitions. (Alternatively, this *could* also be fourth function iNtuition leaping into the superstition, aided by Dominant Sensing skills to put the vitamins in order. We shouldn't be too facile when guessing others' Types!)

IF YOU SUSPECT EVERYTHING,

YOU ARE WASTING MANY SUSPICIONS ON INNOCENT THINGS.

Ashleigh Brilliant

© *Ashleigh Brilliant 1981*   *Pot-Shots No 2216*

This must be explained carefully so you don't hear what we're not saying! Suspicion generally comes from the iNtuitive *function,* whether it be in a Senser or an iNtuitive. (And of course, even paranoids have real enemies.) Paranoia, as Terence Duniho observes,* is the iNtuitive function run amuck. Yet many iNtuitives, particularly iNtuitive Feelers (NFs) are likely to be very trusting. It may be that certain types whose iNtuition is *not* so well developed are most at risk for developing a tendency toward paranoia. While they can be wrong, iNtuitives are likely to be uncannily on target in their suspicions, though they may not know why they feel that way. Note: an Extraverted iNtuitive's *Introverted* iNtuition, when used, is not as good, is less conscious, and more likely to be negative. The reverse is true for Introverted iNtuitives.

* See "Wellness vs. Neurotic Styles: Holistic vs Monomanic Use of the Four Functions," by Terence Duniho, Type & Temperament Press 1992.

Dominant Sensers suffer and benefit from Shadow iNtuition, which gives them unrealistic views of the future (usually negative to disastrous). They expect the worst, and may prepare for disaster, at great expense in current cost and future deprivation. They are the melancholy voice of "doom and gloom."

Dominant Feelers have Shadow Thinking, which fills them with "spurious conclusions," usually negative but based on overgeneralizations and faulty logic.

Dominant Thinkers have Shadow Feeling that can well up from the unconscious and fixate overwhelmingly on an (often inappropriate) person as a love-object. In making values-based decisions, it is not so reliable.

Whenever we're in the *grip* of our Shadow side, it helps to have someone trustworthy with the opposite Dominant function from ourselves to talk to, and provide us with a more realistic picture when we are being fed faulty material from our fourth function.

For *long-term* 4th function growth, work on your less-preferred Attitude: If you're an Extravert, Introvert—i.e., do it alone). If you're an Introvert, Extravert— i.e., do it with a friend). Especially, practice your 4th function in your less-preferred Attitude.

At midlife, as we mature (or at least grow older), we begin developing our "other side" more strongly. Extraverts begin introverting more (if they are to become wholly functioning human beings), and Introverts begin extraverting more (if they are to be truly functional). Otherwise we risk being two-dimensional people, less effective and probably less happy than we might otherwise be. Part of the proverbial 95% of the brain we don't use is simply "aimed the other way."

The chart on page 218-19 summarizes briefly some key effects of the 4th function, ways to deal with it when you are caught in its grip, overreacting or feeling like doing something that's "not you" (i.e., not the conscious you). It also suggests ways to develop your 4th function safely, where it can "play" and not cause trouble.

A single chapter can't cover this subject adequately. You may want to get a book on it, or attend a workshop on the 4th function. It's a lifetime process, making friends with your shadow side. But it's a powerful part of yourself, well worth getting to know!

Chapter 9

Where Do We Go From Here?

I MAY NOT BE TOTALLY PERFECT, BUT PARTS OF ME ARE EXCELLENT.

Pot-Shots No 433

This is it in a nutshell: none of us is perfect, but we all have parts that are excellent— usually our Dominant and Auxiliary functions, the "muscles" we exercise most often. *They* are our "Unfair Advantage."

It's wonderful when you recognize this, and you can design your life to make use of these strengths for your own well-being and for the service of others. And we feel most affirmed and empowered when others recognize us for our best "parts"— our Dominant function.

LIFE IS THE ONLY GAME
IN WHICH THE OBJECT OF THE GAME
IS TO LEARN THE RULES.

© 1975 Ashleigh Brilliant　　　　　　　　　　　　　Pot-Shots No 1409

Really understanding the implications of your best (Dominant) function is like a race-car driver's having an extra passing gear built in, that he didn't realize was there before. Usually our *greatest successes* come from developing and taking advantage of our *Dominant* function— our own "Unfair Advantage."

But we have to have *all four functions* recognized and working well to be a whole person, and achieve true success. Otherwise we will run into problems, be "blindsided" by something relating to a less-preferred function: we just didn't see it coming, as when a Dominant Thinker achieves organizational success— but builds in people problems because he neglects the Feeling side of the operation, and his life. Labor unrest. His kids act out. His wife walks out. As the Pennsylvania Dutch say, "We get too soon old, and too late schmardt!"

Understanding Type gives us the *real* smarts— understanding many of the "rules" of life. It's an Operator's Handbook for this body we were issued when we arrived on earth, red-faced and squalling. If we're lucky, our parents, teachers, mentors, and friends have already taught us a lot of the rules— as they understood them. But learning just a little about Type often provides great new insights— "Aha!" experiences that can suddenly improve the way

224

we function at home and at work. Even a basic knowledge of Type can improve communication, and remove sources of friction and unnecessary conflict.

But it doesn't stop there. The more you learn, the more you will discover; there are depths and subtleties beyond what we can cover in this short book (wait for our next one!). Type is a lifelong journey of discovery. And as you come to master Type (and yourself), your life will truly be a "Hero's Journey."

But enough of that. What are *your* next steps? Like many people, you may say this was a fun book, you learned a lot— and then promptly forget about it. And a month from now you won't be able to remember your 4-letter Type. That's unfortunate, because Type can do so much to improve your life— provided you:

- *Write down* your Type letters. Reread the Type description.
- *Use* Type on a daily basis, at work and at home. *Share* it with family and co-workers. You'll all benefit.
- *Don't stop* now; keep learning.
- *Read* more about Type & Temperament (see book list pg. 241). Attend a seminar on Type.
- Make sure you have correctly identified your *"True Type."* (See page 149)
- *Join* a local Chapter of the international Association for Psychological Type (APT) or other group working with Type.
- *Write* in a journal about your own Type experiences and observations.
- Try some *exercises*, either alone, as couples, as families, or in groups with friends or co-workers. The author and others have developed a number of training materials to help individuals, couples and organizations improve communication and relationships and hone other skills, from conflict reduction to office management and running effective meetings.
- *Make your own Type Table* (see page 151) with your friends' and family's names in the correct block, so you come to know several different examples of each Type. (You may be amazed at how many people you meet already *know* their Type.)
- *Appreciate* the wonderful qualities people of *your same Type* share— and recognize the delightful and unpredictable differ-

ences among them. (We are all different; Type does **not** "put us in boxes," it *frees* us from them.) Type knowledge helps free us from our prejudices and stereotypes.

ALL PEOPLE ARE DIFFERENT. THAT'S WHY EVERYBODY SHOULD BE TREATED THE SAME.

© 1970 Ashleigh Brilliant   Pot-Shots No 222

Dr. Martin Luther King said that race is the *least* significant distinction among different people, and he was right. My colleague Dick Deal says that we really come to appreciate and experience the impact of Type best when we get into a group of strangers all of our own Type. It is a truly empowering experience! You need only meet people of your own Type, but of different racial, ethnic, or social background, or the opposite sex, to know that's true. If we could all come to appreciate that, we would all communicate better, and our nation and our world would overnight be a kinder, gentler place.

It doesn't matter what Type you are; being with a group of folks like yourself is a powerful experience. And when you see groups of *other* Types and can compare how differently you each operate, the learning is unforgettable. We all need to learn truly to appreciate others for their *different* strengths and styles.

The Golden Rule of Type— We all know the Golden Rule— "Do unto others as you would have others do unto you." George Bernard Shaw (probably an INTJ) said, "Do *not* do unto others as you would that they should do unto you. Their tastes may not be the same." Type knowledge refines that to, "Do unto others as you would have them do unto you— *if you were their Type!*"

Applications of Type go wide and deep. Type is a powerful tool in communication, teambuilding, couples counseling, education, medicine, law, administration and organizational development. It is used in churches and the military, by social workers and therapists and corporate managers. In short, Type can improve the way any two people communicate, work or live together, negotiate, argue, sell, hold meetings, make love, plan vacations, or just about anything else humans do. A few examples might help.

A *college* began using Type to match up roommates; complaints dropped 50%.

Books and training materials have been developed to relate Type to countless specific applications: career selection; the law; teaching styles; writing styles; architecture and space use; sales; couples counseling; surviving midlife; spiritual growth; addiction and codependency; dropout reduction; and more are being developed as we write.

Local school districts have used Type to improve teaching— so teachers can *teach children the way the children learn*, not the way that teacher naturally tends to teach. Type knowledge can also improve relationships between faculty and administrative staff, and with parents and school boards.

Some *judges* use Type to be aware of their own natural biases when rendering decisions that might reflect differing viewpoints— e.g., Introverts are generally more concerned than Extraverts about privacy rights. (Especially important with judges of rare Types.)

Attorneys use Type in law office management, dealing with staff and clients, case presentation, jury selection, conflict reduction, and improving communication— in the firm, and with clients, juries and judges. Also in terms of deciding their legal specialty, e.g., Feelers often prefer different specialties from Thinkers.

Advertisers use Type to understand their best customers and their needs, so they can design products to serve and appeal better to them and design advertising that will speak more clearly and convincingly to the *kinds of people* who are their heaviest users. Smart agencies cast their commercials, and design their copy strategy to aim their advertising at their best customers. Type enables them to do that far more effectively.

227

Salespersons use Type to communicate more effectively with their customers and prospects. You can sell most easily to someone of your own Type; communication is then natural and enjoyable. With other Types, it pays to "style-shift" so you can deliver the message you intend, in a way that it will be correctly heard and best received. One technical manufacturer's CEO was a rare "1%" Type, and "cloned" himself in selecting sales representatives: most were his own rare Type. He sold them on his product line; but they had to work harder to sell it to customers, since most were other Types. Understanding themselves made it easier for them to sell *all* their product lines. The CEO was encouraged to diversify his selection process, since sales skills were not his strong suit.

Many *career counselors* use Type to help clients, students, and persons in transition to find the most suitable career path for their own skills and preferences. We all tend to self-select careers based on our Type; that's why we think of a particular style when we hear the words, "accountant-Type," or "lawyer-Type," or "used car salesman-Type"— all different images, or stereotypes, but with some factual basis, i.e., Typology. While every career has some of every Type, and nearly anyone can do well in a career if they are motivated enough, there are some fields that will be easier for you— if only because most people in that field are your Type, so communication will be easier. In a field where you are unusual, you may have more unique things to contribute— but may find it harder to do so. Also, come downsizing time, unless you have a specialty, you *may* be among the first to go if you are not like the others!

Many *therapists* know and use Type to understand and to help establish rapport with clients, to help identify and define the extent of the problem, and to help improve relationships, as in couples and family counseling. Also, if they *do* have a serious problem, some Types may be more likely to have certain problems than others. Type is also useful in pairing clients with therapists in industry or group practices, and knowing your Type may be useful for you in selecting a counselor.(There are pluses and minuses to working with a counselor who's just your Type: easy communication and trust, but tends to have the same blind spots) vs one who is your opposite (may have a sharper view of your problems, but be harder to trust and communicate with, and you may resist therapy).

Conclusion

Don't miss the *important information* in the Appendix (that's Latin for "no pictures"). The Energy-direction material is very powerful; although a bit sophisticated, it can be extremely helpful. The "Caveats On Type™" or "Things to Watch Out For" are vital and everyone should read them. Bottom line is, don't go off and make sudden radical changes in your life based on this one book— or any other. Use your Perceiving (even if you're a Judger) and get more information. And check out your *preferred* mode of deciding (Thinking or Feeling) with one or more trusted friends, pastor, counselor who's strong on the *other* side, who knows Type, and who knows you.

Jung said the word was "balance." You may now know your 4-letter Type preference. But don't forget the other 4 letters hiding in your Shadow. They're less developed—like little children, but with powerful weapons. They love you, and want to help you, too.

But with all this emphasis on the 4th function and the shadow side, be sure *first* to tend to your Dominant, most-preferred function, *and* your Auxiliary (which many of us don't use enough).

The first and greatest contribution of Type is usually in clearly recognizing our Dominant and its strengths. This is the "Aha!" experience of truly seeing ourselves for the first time, and appreciating ourselves for who we really are. Only then can we be most effective in life. The Dominant is our "money function," on which most successful careers are based.

The second powerful contribution of Type is in recognizing the importance of developing our balancing Auxiliary, which (inconveniently, but necessarily) operates in our less-preferred direction. If we are Extraverts, we must find quiet time to use it; if we are Introverts, we must play Extravert to benefit from our Auxiliary.

Understanding and developing the third and fourth functions, and ultimately all the other parts of ourselves, is the third contribution of Type. It is not a magic solution; it's more like the key to a great gate, and when we enter we have begun a lifelong journey in a land more wonderful than we could have imagined, with powers greater than we could have dreamed. Enjoy!

Appendix I— Energy Direction

Perhaps one of the most important and least understood concepts in Type is energy flow. As we've seen, we can direct our energy two ways: outward, into the world of people, places and things (Extravertedly); or inward, within ourselves, into the inner world of ideas and concepts and inner images (Introvertedly). We have a basic preference for either Introversion or Extraversion.

But each of our four *functions*— two ways of perceiving: Sensing and iNtuition, and two ways of deciding: Thinking and Feeling— has a *preferred direction* of its own, either Extraverted or Introverted. Normally two functions face in each direction, to give balance. We have a favorite *Introverted* way of perceiving and deciding, and a favorite *Extraverted* way of perceiving and deciding. If our Sensing is Extraverted, our iNtuition is Introverted, and vice versa. If our Thinking is Introverted, our Feeling is Extraverted, and vice versa. This pattern is not random, but is specific to each Type. (For each Type, the chart on page 233 shows in which direction you normally use each function.)

The diagram on page 232 illustrates the general case:

1. We use our *favorite function* in our *favorite world:*
   • Extraverts Extravert their Dominant function,
   • Introverts Introvert their Dominant function.

2. We use our *Auxiliary (#2) function in our #2 world:*
   • Extraverts Introvert their Auxiliary function,
   • Introverts Extravert their Auxiliary function.

3. *Balance* is the ruling principle. If we Extravert a function, we Introvert its opposite, and vice versa.
   • If we Extravert Sensing, we Introvert iNtuition, and vice versa
   • If we Extravert Thinking, we Introvert Feeling, and vice versa

4. Simply put,
   • Extraverts Extravert #1 and #3, and Introvert #2 and #4
   • Introverts Introvert #1 and #3, and Extravert #2 and #4.*

* Note to Jungians: Of course, we all use *all four* functions, and use each at times in *each* direction. We are talking of *preferences,* and of relative strength due to more frequent use of preferred functions and directions. There is a sentence in Jung that implies a different direction for the third function, i.e., that Extraverts Extravert #1, and Introvert the other three functions, while Introverts Introvert #1,

To add another layer of subtlety, a function is *qualitatively different*, depending upon whether it is Introverted or Extraverted. Extraverts generally act faster, for better or for worse, and so do Extraverted *functions*, even for an Introvert. However, an Extravert's two *Introverted* functions take longer to operate. Even for Dominant Feelers, if that Dominant Feeling is *Introverted* (as with INFP and ISFP), they will need processing time for decision-making. Let them sleep on it; don't expect the quick decisions you hear from *Extraverted* Dominant Feelers (ESFJ and ENFJ). The same is true of Dominant Thinkers (Introverted— INTP and ISTP, vs. Extraverted— ENTJ and ESTJ).

But there is more than a time difference; there is a real qualitative distinction. Extraversion and Introversion are "Attitudes." While Introverts do spend most of the time with their mouths closed, Extraverts don't always have theirs open (it just seems that way to Introverts). Extraversion approaches things with the question, "How do *I* relate to t*hat?*" Introversion approaches the same things with the question, "How does *that* relate to *me*? Or does it?" It is beyond the scope of this basic book to get into detailed pictures of these differences, but be aware that there *are* differences!

and Extravert the other three. This "one vs. three" (as opposed to the more balanced "2 vs. 2") has not been our experience, and most Type experts agree. Jung did not have the advantage of the present widespread interest in and use of Type; his subjects were chiefly his patients, not the general population. He defined only 8 Types, and he did not have the fourth letter (J/P) or the statistical data, both developed by Myers. In fact, Jung did not continue to focus on Type, but became interested in other areas, though he still considered Type important. Lastly, in all his writing on Type, *balance* was of primary importance. But, for example, an Extraverted Perceiver who had no Extraverted judging function with which to express decisions would not be a balanced individual. So much for theory. Most convincing to me is my own observation and experience with well persons. The two and two model appears to reflect how most people usually work in the real world, though there is latitude for individual variation due to differences in environment and upbringing, and some still dispute this point.

Energy Flow by Psychological Type

The General Model:

Function

Dominant

Auxiliary

Tertiary

Least-Preferred

EXTRAVERT

Internal Focus

External Appearance

INTROVERT

Internal Focus

Function

Dominant

Auxiliary

Tertiary

Least-Preferred

Functions normally Extraverted point outward
Functions normally Introverted point inward

Extraverts tend to extravert their #1 & #3 functions, and introvert their #2 & #4

Introverts tend to introvert their #1 & #3 functions, and extravert their #2 & #4

Energy Direction

Order of Preference of The 4 Functions
for the 16 types*

Order:	1 (Dominant)	2 (Auxiliary)	3 (Tertiary)	4 ("Shadow")
Types				
I**S**TJ	S_i	T_e	F_i	N_e
I**S**FJ	S_i	F_e	T_i	N_e
I**N**FJ	N_i	F_e	T_i	S_e
I**N**TJ	N_i	T_e	F_i	S_e
IS**T**P	T_i	S_e	N_i	F_e
IS**F**P	F_i	S_e	N_i	T_e
IN**F**P	F_i	N_e	S_i	T_e
IN**T**P	T_i	N_e	S_i	F_e
E**S**TP	S_e	T_i	F_e	N_i
E**S**FP	S_e	F_i	T_e	N_i
E**N**FP	N_e	F_i	T_e	S_i
E**N**TP	N_e	T_i	F_e	S_i
ES**T**J	T_e	S_i	N_e	F_i
ES**F**J	F_e	S_i	N_e	T_i
EN**F**J	F_e	N_i	S_e	T_i
EN**T**J	T_e	N_i	S_e	F_i

(Dominant [#1] Function is underlined. The subscript "e" or "i" indicates whether the function is usually Extraverted or Introverted for each type— though at times we all use each of the 4 functions both ways! See discussion of energy flows and diagram.)

Appendix II

It Started With Hippocrates—
A Brief History of Type

The ancient Greek Hippocrates (he of the Hippocratic Oath which medical doctors take) tells us of 4 Temperaments (called "humors"): Choleric, Melancholic, Sanguine & Phlegmatic, each a recognizable personality style. Everyone seemed to fit pretty well one or another. It was helpful to understand people, and for millenia educated people learned these 4 categories as a "given." Paracelsus (16th century) likened the 4 styles to different animals/kinds of mythical beings: nymphs, sylphs, gnomes and salamanders. Shakespeare used his knowledge of temperament to good advantage, creating unforgettable characters, precisely since they are typologically accurate. The "melancholy Jacques" *was* a Melancholic. The 17th and 18th century English poets, steeped in classical literature, assumed each of us reflected one of the 4 Temperaments.

Then came the Age of Reason. The Enlightenment, Scientific Rationalism, which of course first attracted the naturally scientific Types, the Phlegmatics. The mellow poetical types, also iNtuitive, adapted to the new vocabulary (17th century metaphysical poets used scientific terms to talk of love, lust and theology) but it took some time for them to let go of the basic, practical understanding of human Temperament. As science grew in the 18th century, new discoveries shook us to our roots.

Scientific methods were applied to the improvement of man as well as machine. Freudian principles made little use of the quaint old notions of Temperament. In the "Nature vs Nurture" argument, Nurture carried the day, perhaps since it's easier to sell services based on a perfectible person model (Be whatever you desire) than on unchangeable nature (Be what you're best suited to be). (As always, truth, in the middle, gets oversimplified out of the picture.)

But Carl Jung, heir-apparent to Freud, split with the master. He had observed basic Type differences among his patients and friends. In 1920 he wrote "Psychological Types," and Extraverts and Introverts became the rage. He identified Thinkers and Feelers, and Sensers and iNtuitives, but these were not so widely popularized. Earlier (1907), Adickes had written of the 4 Temperaments

234

as Dogmatic, Agnostic, Traditional, and Novative. About the same time as Jung (1920), Spranger and Kretschmer were separately renaming the 4 Temperaments they observed.

In the US, two women who were *not* psychologists made a breakthrough. They dealt daily with normal people, and developed a "well person" instrument to determine Type. Katherine Briggs had been developing a theory of Type, and when she read of Jung's work, she adopted his terminology and approach. Unfortunately, Jung failed to pursue his excellent work on Type. He did not develop an instrument to identify people's Types. Briggs and her daughter, Isabel Briggs Myers, did. They added the concept of Judgers and Perceivers (which Jung implied but did not explicitly incorporate) to Jung's three pairs, and the 4-pair system of sixteen 4-letter Types was born. After years of development and testing at Educational Testing Service in Princeton, their instrument was made generally available in 1975, published and promoted by CPP in California.

David Keirsey, a psychologist working with Temperament, read Myers' work and related her 16 Types effectively to the 4 Temperaments. Most psychologists and psychiatrists have been slow to adopt Type, perhaps because many were Freudians, disapproved of Jung, and could not accept an instrument developed by two women who were not psychologists. Career counselors, business people, educators, clergy, the military, and many others have adopted Type with great success because *it works*.

Measurement of Type— Personality Tests

There are hundreds of personality tests, many designed to measure pathology, most focused on a single aspect (e.g. Extraversion, or Extraversion-Introversion).

The Myers-Briggs Type Indicator® (MBTI®)* is by far the most widely used instrument for determining Type. With *any* Type indicator, especially if your scores are at all close, you may want to follow up with a professional to get assistance in determining your "True Type." We have our own Bill Murray Type Checklist™ (Chapter 6) to give you a quick picture of your preferences. Dozens of others have developed their own questionnaires to measure the basic Jungian categories and/or the 4 Temperaments, sometimes for specific situations such as education or management. Often they use new names to differentiate their format, e.g., analytical, managerial; or eagles, bears, foxes and owls. Some Type indicators are better than others, but none should

* Myers-Briggs Type Indicator® and MBTI® are registered trademarks of Consulting Psychologists Press.

be used blindly; after you determine your style according to an indicator, check it out carefully with a set of good Type descriptions to be sure you agree with the results. You are the best judge of who you are, not some paper self-report form, not someone else (though their input may be helpful).

If you would like to change some aspects of yourself, that's fine. We are all growing and developing. But you can grow better and more effectively if you start by understanding clearly just who you are now. That's what this book is all about. You will always *be* your True Type, but you can learn to develop all 8 letters to achieve a better balance and live your life more effectively. You can change your *behavior*, and you can develop new *skills*.

Appendix III

CAVEATS ON TYPE

(Things to Watch Out For)

1. We all use all Functions and Attitudes, every day.
2. There are **no** "good" or "bad" Types.
3. The Myers-Briggs Type Indicator® (MBTI®)—or any other psychological instrument—should not be the sole basis for any major decision.
4. Type is a *dynamic*, not a static factor. A process, not a diagnosis. People do change in some situations (stress, "passages," environment, developmental stages.)
5. Though "true Type" does not change, it may be **masked** by situational factors. Furthermore, we do not always behave "according to Type." We have the option to use the function most appropriate to the situation, even if it is not a preferred function. If we try, we can improve the ability to use each of our four functions as necessary.
6. There are wide individual variations within each Type.
7. Specific numbers or scores are meaningless in themselves. (A zero on "T" doesn't mean one can't think, nor does a zero "F" mean one has no feelings. A "30" iNtuitive is not necessarily more creative than a "10" iNtuitive.) High scores indicate a strong preference— not necessarily high skill in that area, nor low development in its opposite. Close scores don't imply strength

in both letters. They may indicate tension or conflict around a pair of functions, e.g., whether to use "F" or "T."

8. We all have a *bias* as we speak, while we listen, and when we respond. This is natural. Type increases our awareness of such biases and enables us to compensate appropriately for them.

9. Psychological Type—though it is a very powerful tool—is not *everything*. Other factors also affect our personalities: values, motivation, age, sex, birth order, intelligence, and much more.

10. Differences between males and females of the same Type may be due in part to societal influences.

11. Type Indicators are *self-report* instruments and thus are subject to error. *You* are the best judge of your True Type. It may take some time to be sure; that's only normal.

12. The **motivation** of the person taking the inventory can influence the answers.

13. It is unwise to use the MBTI (or any personality style indicator) for selection purposes (of mates, employees, etc.)

14. Personality testing is definitely not an exact science. Measurement error and lack of precision are inevitable in all personality instruments.

15. This material does not represent (nor is it intended to be) an in-depth study of Type. It is meant to be an *introduction*. The study of personality Type is an exciting, lifelong effort.

About the Author

William D.G. Murray, true to his Type, has had a variety of successful careers: Air Force officer, magazine editor, university instructor in English and physics, marketing & advertising executive, corporate president and director, entrepreneur, consultant and seminar leader on psychological Type and temperament, poet, author, and publisher.

Murray served in various positions with Eastman Kodak and later Procter & Gamble, in the brand management area, where he worked on eight different brands. Next he became one of three stockholders in Weightman, Inc, a small Philadelphia advertising agency where he handled a little-known regional dog food: ALPO. In seven years the brand was #1 in the US, more than double #2, and Murray was Sr VP, Managing Director, and Director of Account Service at the city's second-largest agency. With a partner he started General Ecology, Inc., and began manufacturing Seagull® drinking water purifiers, a decade before most people became aware of the need for better water.

He was also early in discovering the power of psychological Type. At a church conference in the 70's, "I learned more about myself in one morning than in all the years I'd lived." At the time there were no books on Type as we now know it. Murray dug up articles, dissertations, and other papers on the subject, attended seminars, met the leaders in the field, and was a founding member of the Association for Psychological Type (APT) when it was formed, in Philadelphia (1979). He has served on the Board and as an officer of the Northeast Region of APT, and President of the Delaware Valley chapter. As well as contributing to national publications in the field, with his wife, Rosalie, he is author of several books, a number of widely used training materials, and complete seminar kits for Type professionals: Type & Teambuilding, Type Communication, Type & Your Career, Introduction to Psychological Type, Thinkers & Feelers, and more.

A recognized leader in the field of Type, Murray has presented at regional, national and foreign conferences. He is now President of Type & Temperament, Inc, a Gladwyne, PA firm specializing in practical applications of personality Type, in two areas: (1) Publishing— books and training materials; and (2) Consulting, Education & Training, in-house & on-site, for organizations couples and individuals.

About the Illustrator

Ashleigh Brilliant

"True wit is Nature to advantage dress'd,
What oft was thought, but ne'er so well
express'd."
Alexander Pope—Essay on Criticism, Part II, line 97

Pope defined it nicely. Ashleigh Brilliant's epigrams are "true wit," and he is now running a close second to Mark Twain as the most quoted source in the Readers Digest's "Quotable Quotes."

To answer your question, Ashleigh Brilliant *is* his real name. Born in England, of Brilliant parents, in 1933, he spent 1941-46 in Washington DC, where his father was a civilian member of the British Admiralty delegation. He returned to England for his education through college. He has had a fascinating career.

He gave a public speech on Human Rights in Moscow in 1959; Russia expelled him. "Publicly designated a 'hippie' by the San Francisco *Examiner* (1967)," he taught in the California school system, and the "Floating University." He holds degrees from three universities, including a Ph.D. in history from U. C. Berkeley.

Dr. Brilliant began in the 1960's, at others' behest, to write down the *bon mots* that came naturally to his speech. The shoebox soon overflowed. He gave readings of them to friends, calling them "Unpoemed Titles." Suggestions that he illustrate them eventually led to the idea of publishing them as postcards, which could be *used* as well as read. In a sense, this was a totally new form of literature. Dr. Brilliant has seriously (if amusingly) created an ongoing series— thousands of what he calls "Pot-Shots®"

Since so many of his works are (individual) postcards, there are now over 100 million in print, which may make him the most published author in history. Seldom has an author had such salutary effect on so many lives; these greetings have added much cheer to millions of people, and lubrication to their relationships. They are also published in books— see page 244 for a list.

His Pot-Shots display incredible understanding of the human character and condition, and many are (he might be surprised to hear it said), truly spiritual in content, if not content in their spirituality. Though he may never become Pope, he will always remain truly Brilliant.

A Word About the Pot-Shots®

Though it may not be readily apparent, there *is* a structure—some rules—underlying the Pot-Shots®. First is *Brevity:* no longer than 17 words. [Because at the time he began formulating rules, he had already formulated many Pot-Shots®, and the longest was 17 words. Also, Japanese Haiku poetry uses exactly 17 syllables (not words). So 17 it is.]

Second principle is *universality:* ever the iNtuitive global thinker, from the start he decided to avoid puns, rhymes, word-play or references unique to one language or culture, and to use only simple, common, easily translated words. This put a premium on "irony, ambiguity, subtlety, audacity, paradox and crazy logic."

Third is *originality*; though they must *sound* like everyday speech, they must not *be* something said before. As Shakespeare might have said (but didn't), "The *word's* the thing." The *illustration* is incidental (though often adds greatly to the impact, given the old rule about how many words a [well-chosen] picture is worth). Ashleigh's delightful illustrations are worth their weight in—words.

A Word About Copyrights

Ashleigh's words, by the way, are some of the most valuable in history, based on how much he has been paid (with court assistance) by those illegally appropriating them, including *Time* magazine and Universal Studios, foreign corporations as well as larcenous individuals with copiers.

Each Pot-Shot® is individually copyrighted, and **since they are his livelihood, he has from the start pursued a policy of assiduously protecting them, regardless of cost or time involved. The courts have ruled consistently that they are, though very short, in fact fully protected.** "Once again," as Ashleigh put it so well, "justice has triumphed over piracy on the high ©'s." (IFMB pg 13). Stealing copyrighted material is not only criminal activity and likely to be costly; it's *unkind* to the writer.

Or to spell it out the way an earlier Author put it, **"Thou shalt not steal."**

Other Books and Materials by William D. G. Murray—BOOKS

And You Didn't Think You Had a Prayer, by Wm. D. G. Murray. Sixteen serious prayers for the 16 Types. Memorable, insightful, these will speak to you. There's one for you, and each of your friends and family. *"You have touched my very soul. I'm giving this to all my friends"* **When ENFP & INFJ Interact,** by William D.G. Murray and Rosalie R. Murray (also available on cassette). This neat little book *tells you more about INFJs than anything we've seen,* regardless of the Types with which they frequently interact. But of course, this is primarily an in-depth review of these two Types and how they interact with each other. Includes sections on Love, Sex & Relationships; Attitudes Toward Money; Child-rearing; Recreation & Vacations; INFJ Careers; INFJ Boss with ENFP Employee (and vice-versa); INFJs in Therapy (very helpful information) and more. **OPPOSITES: When ENFP & ISTJ Interact,** by William D.G. Murray and Rosalie R. Murray. *Tells you more about ENFPs and more about ISTJs than anything we've seen.* Similar topics to ENFP/INFJ above, including Careers for ISTJs and ISTJs in Therapy. Focused on these two Types, but provides useful information for any of the 8 pairs of opposites. Gives both positive and negative aspects, subtle benefits and subtle problems as well as the more obvious ones. Readers' comments: *"Far less expensive than an hour of counseling," "You saved our marriage." "This really helped me understand my boss."*

Complete Seminar Presentation Kits for Trainers, Consultants , Educators and Counselors
To present Type to groups, couples, or individual clients, in an organized and professional style
(Overheads, Speaker's script/notes, & Handouts)

- **Introduction to Psychological Type**
- **Type Communication**
- **Feelers and Thinkers**
- **Opposites**
- **Type & Teambuilding**
- **Type & Careers**

Workshop & Counseling Materials & Tapes

1. The **Type Communications**™ Materials—contains 4 materials: (Caveats on Type; Type Basics; Prescriptions for Extraverts (and Introverts, Sensors, et al); When Extravert & Introvert Relate (and E with E; I with I: S with N, etc.) Also available on audiocassette.
2. **Reframing** — Type, Temperament and Cognitive Therapy— Helps reduce unnecessary conflict.
3. **Key Words in Type-** for E,I,S,N,T,F,J,&P
4. **Type & Law Office Management—** by William D. G. Murray & Frank L. Natter, P.A.- Audiotape & Materials- Helpful for any

situation where Client, Staff, and Professional must interact.

     5. **Type & Case Presentation,** William D.G. Murray & Frank L. Natter, P.A. - Audiotape & Materials

     6. **Type Speculations on Jury Selection,** Natter &Murray

     7. **Energy Flow Templates**, — Diagrams of Type Interactions —William D.G. Murray & Peter Walsh

Other Type-Related Books & Materials from Type & Temperament, Inc. —BOOKS:

Discover the Power of Introversion: What Most Introverts Are Never Told, and Extraverts Learn the Hard Way, by Cheryl N. W. Card. Great little book helps Introverts appreciate themselves (helps Extraverts understand and appreciate Introverts, too). And helps Extraverts recognize the need to develop their own (Introverted) Auxiliary function so they can be whole and effective in day-to-day situations and relationships.

The Way of the Cross: Christian Individuation and Psychological Temperament, by Richard D. Grant, Jr., PhD. Grant relates the Jungian Typological quaternity and Temperament to the 4 Gospel traditions, the epistles, and numerous Christian traditions including the Angelus, the Eucharist, and the Stations of the Cross. A thoughtful and helpful guide for study, worship and personal growth. Useful for non-Catholics (and even non-Christians) as well as Catholics since his focus is universal, not parochial.

The I Ching: Images of Psychological Typology and Development, by Richard D. Grant, Jr., PhD. The ancient Chinese I Ching, with 64 symbols (hexagrams) and accompanying text and metaphors, used for ages as an oracle, has a worldview of counterbalanced masculine (yang) and feminine (yin) forces as the basis of all growth and movement. Its advice is timeless, remarkably modern because it is archetypal. Relates the I Ching to the 16 Types, 4 Temperaments, archetypes, and Erik Erikson's stages of psychosocial development.

Symbols of Recovery: The 12 Steps at Work in the Unconscious, by Richard D. Grant, Jr., Ph.D. Explores close connection between the process of recovery as experienced in the 12-step programs and transformation of the deep psyche as explained by both therapeutic modes & spiritual traditions. Correlates the 12-step process with other Symbol Systems that map the spiritual changes deep in the psyche: the "hero's journey" in mythology, the Zodiac, Alchemy processes (symbols used by Jung in therapy) and Tarot cards.

Each system is then translated into extremely helpful process questions or exercises based on the 12-steps program.

Making Good Decisions by Terence Duniho— A brief look at Type & decision-making by groups & individuals.

Your Shadow Side—The Fourth Function: Achilles' Heel and Pearl of Great Price, by Terence Duniho — Recommended reading for all Type-people. A very good review of key effects of the energy of our Fourth Function, the vital necessary weakling that gets us into such unexpected trouble, or shows us the way to great spiritual insights. Some worthwhile observations relating to stress, behavior modification, and more.

"Personalities at Risk: Addiction, Codependency and Psychological Type" by Terence Duniho — Duniho relates Type/Temperament to addiction and codependency. Useful insights on the importance of the Feeling function in addictive behavior. Covers closed vs. open systems, process addictions and Type, fears and unmet needs, and suggested solutions. A unique contribution.

"Wholeness Lies Within: Sixteen Natural Paths Toward Spirituality," by Terence Duniho —Thoughtful volume looks at some of the "Big" questions. Designed "to provide intellectual underpinnings for the person who seeks truth that works, but doesn't want to blindly accept religious dogma" ... and "for the person, like myself, raised with a Judeo-Christian perspective, who up 'til now has not been able to usefully apply that perspective to their own life."

"Wellness vs. Neurotic Styles: Holistic vs Monomanic Use of the 4 Functions," by Terence Duniho— We risk potential problems when we fail to develop one of our 4 functions (S, N, T & F). Understanding Type can help us avoid dysfunction in ourselves and misdiagnosis of others. Helps us deal with stress, achieve wellness.

Workshop & Counseling Materials & Tapes

Type Prayers by Ellis Harsham

Type Dynamics by Peter Walsh

Decision - Making from the Dominant Function— Peter Walsh

Teaching to Type — Dennis Campbell

Planning Productive Meetings Using Psychological Type- A Checklist — Marthanne Luzader

The 4 Temperaments— George Schemel

Temperament Quiz— Judith Roemer

Temperament Management Quiz— Judith Roemer

Type-Law Tapes — 5 tapes by Frank L. Natter, P.A.

Personal Problem-Solving — 4 tapes by Frank L. Natter, P.A.

Problem- Solving in Relationships — 3 tapes by F.L. Natter

By the time you read this, perhaps more ...

We also offer an extensive catalogue of Type-related books and materials from other publishers for your convenience. T&T Inc.'s seminar division offers workshops and training for organizations, couples, and individuals, both in house and in our facilities.

We will be happy to send you a catalogue or listing of our latest publications and workshops.

Please send a stamped self-addressed envelope to:

Type & Temperament Inc.
PO Box 200
Gladwyne PA 19035-0200 USA
Or just call Toll Free: 1-(800) IHS-TYPE
[1-800-447-8973]   [outside USA call (610) 527-2330]
FAX (610) 527-1722FAX

Other Books by Ashleigh Brilliant

Dr. Brilliant has written 8 volumes of Pot-Shots®, and one volume of essays and poems:

BOOKS OF POT-SHOTS®

1. I May Not Be Totally Perfect, But Parts of Me Are Excellent

2. I Have Abandoned My Search for Truth, and Am Now Looking for a Good Fantasy

3. I Feel Much Better Now That I've Given Up Hope

4. Appreciate Me Now and Avoid the Rush

5. All I Want Is a Warm Bed, a Kind Word, and Unlimited Power

6. I Try to Take One Day At a Time, But Sometimes Several Days Attack Me At Once

7. We've Been Through So Much Together, And Most Of It Was Your Fault

8. I Want To Reach Your Mind— Where Is It Currently Located?

ESSAYS AND POEMS

Be A Good Neighbor and Leave Me Alone

All are published by Woodbridge Press, and are also available from:
Type & Temperament, Inc,
P.O. Box 200,
Gladwyne PA 19035-0200 USA

Or call 1- (800) IHS-TYPE

Overseas call (610) 527-2330
FAX (610) 527-1722

Notes

Notes